The Grammar of Romance

A Comparative Introduction to Vulgar Latin & the Romance Languages

Joshua Rudder

Contents

Introduction

Quid est soloecismus? Oratio Latinis quidem verbis, verum vitiosa conpositione prolata.

What is a grammatical error? Speaking with Latin words but flawed structure.

Victorinus, *De soloecismo et barbarismo*

The book in your hands introduces the basic grammar of Vulgar Latin and its modern descendants. It compares and contrasts related languages, presents general trends throughout the Romance family and calls attention to significant divergences. It's a reference for learners or enthusiasts of the Romance languages, including students pursuing multiple Romance languages, linguistically inclined individuals and speakers of one of the languages looking to expand their understanding of the family.

This entire work is built upon and organized around examples. The main chapters and supplementary tables offer lots of examples from specific languages and use multiple languages to highlight each topic. Explanations wrap these examples in text that abstracts grammatical concepts and makes particular points about Romance grammar. Together, the examples and explanations are clustered by grammatical topic, beginning with individual nouns and verbs and progressing all the way to simple and compound sentences.

Extra materials beyond the main text and tables include a brief pronunciation guide and a quick overview of Vulgar Latin grammar that distills common Romance features. A topical index at the very end of the book helps you locate major concepts and key terms.

A COMPARATIVE GRAMMAR OF ROMANCE?

Briefly, a grammar shares how a language works. A Romance grammar shares how the Romance languages work. This comparative grammar introduces Vulgar Latin and the modern

Romance languages in parallel, comparing related languages instead of focusing on a single language.

The Romance languages are a family of languages that descend from Latin. The Romans spread Latin as they conquered their way across Europe. Separate dialects developed in different places, and these dialects eventually split into distinct languages. The five major Romance languages—Spanish, French, Portuguese, Italian and Romanian—all trace their ancestry to Latin. Many more local and regional languages trace their roots back to Latin, such as Catalan, Sicilian, Romansh and Sardinian.

A form of Vulgar Latin, not Classical Latin, is the reconstructed parent of the modern Romance languages. Reconstruction relies on facts in evidence from later languages to isolate features inherited from an earlier language. Vulgar Latin presumably witnessed an array of variants with many competing features, but only those features common to Proto-Romance survived. We may infer that Vulgar Latin was not confined to Proto-Romance; however, its unrecorded words and words that continue into none of the successor languages remain casualties of language history.

HOW THIS BOOK IS ORGANIZED

This grammar strives to be readily approachable, intuitive and unenigmatic. If you find that you need explicit instructions to make sense of the layout and formatting, I have failed in that goal. Still, several remarks about the structure of this book are warranted for clarity's sake.

Taking the wide view, this grammar is divided into the main text (chapters on nouns, verbs, etc.) and the supplementary materials (like the tables and pronunciation guide). The main text splits into chapters, sections and subsections, each with its own heading. For instance, the first chapter on nouns has a section on noun gender with a subsection on feminine nouns.

The body of this handbook showcases the major traits of Romance grammar. Because of that focus, examples neglect thorough coverage in favor of illustration. For more thorough (but still basic) data, see the supplementary grammar tables, which are meant to complement the main text.

FORMATTING OF THE EXPLANATIONS & EXAMPLES

Each grammar topic explored in the text corresponds to a key term. Topics explained and exemplified in a specific section are formatted as _emphatic key terms_. Topics simply referenced in one section but explained in another are formatted as <u>cross-referenced key terms</u>. The use of key terms in this text resembles hyperlinks in a webpage, offering an immediate path to track down related topics. The topical index and table of contents support searches for cross-referenced key terms and topics.

This text is littered with examples from Latin and the Romance languages. Examples and translations always appear in emphatic print, with translations following the examples: **example** _translation_. The name of the source language precedes examples from that language: Portuguese **língua**, Catalan **llengua**, Sardinian **limba** _language_.

The asterisk symbol (*) is overloaded in this handbook, but the line between its two uses is cut clearly. Most Latin examples begin with an asterisk, which signifies that they come from a largely undocumented form of the language called Vulgar Latin, the popular spoken language of the late Roman Empire: Classical Latin **loquor** translates _I speak_, but some Vulgar Latin speakers used ***parabolo** instead. Latin examples are typically followed by modern Romance examples: Vulgar Latin ***lingua**, Portuguese **língua**, Catalan **llengua**, Sardinian **limba** _language_.

A non-Latin example begins with an asterisk when it contains negative evidence, demonstrating what speakers are not likely to say or write. For instance, an English speaker would probably not write _*the Robert's language_ for _Robert's language_. Of course, there are infinitely many random things speakers do not say for a given phrase—not surprisingly, the string *zwqwkzz doesn't appear in Romance. I bring up certain negative examples to highlight unused or little-used words and phrases that you could reasonably expect speakers of a language to say. I place negative examples next to positive ones for comparison. This admittedly informal process has the virtue of inviting you to search the internet and other resources for parallel structures and check for yourself.

The sign > marks a derivation. The word on the right side of the sign comes from the word on the left: Vulgar Latin *lingua > Sardinian limba means that the Latin word *lingua became the Sardinian word limba. If the sign is reversed, so is the derivational path: Sardinian limba < Vulgar Latin *lingua.

The text avoids abbreviations like pl. for plural, ind. for indicative or m. for masculine. These kinds of shortened forms do appear when they save vital space, particularly in cramped tables.

Translations attempt to reproduce both the meaning and the structure of their source examples. Parentheses tend to mark helpful comments in a translation: Italian Lei *you (formal)* indicates that the Italian word Lei addresses someone in a polite manner. Less frequently, parentheses surround optional material: Romanian e(ste) *is* suggests that Romanian speakers say either e or este where English speakers use *is*. Square brackets mark material inserted into the translation but not present in the source language: Latin linguam *[the] language* expresses that the Classical Latin example lacks a definite article where English allows or prefers it.

Slashes signal a choice between multiple examples or translations. When two words are immediately separated by an adjacent slash, the slash marks a choice between the two individual words: Vulgar Latin *nostra lingua *our language/tongue* shows that the word lingua corresponds to the word *language* and the word *tongue*. When spaces surround the slash, it marks a choice between multi-word phrases: French on parle *we speak / it is spoken* shows that the French phrase translates to English *we speak* or *it is spoken*.

Examples also appear in tables within the main text and in the supplementary material. The following table compares the Vulgar Latin and Romance words for *language* to demonstrate the look and layout of tables.

language	example
Vulgar Latin	***lingua**
Portuguese	**língua**
Catalan	**llengua**
Sardinian	**limba**
	language

The index at the end of this book focuses on general grammatical topics rather than words and structures in individual languages. This mirrors the main text, which showcases examples from a variety of languages at every turn and rarely digs much deeper into a specific language. To learn how the regular Vulgar Latin verb ***amare** works, you might search for <u>verbs</u>, <u>tenses</u> or <u>moods</u>, but you would not have the same success searching under ***amare**. Language-specific words of grammatical interest are included, such as Vulgar Latin ***quod**, French **on**, Venetian **drio**, Occitan **pas**, Romanian **să** and Spanish **estar**, but general grammar terms are the real stars of the index.

With this information in hand, you're equipped to read through this handbook as well as the online version of this grammar (www.nativlang.com/romance-languages).

Nouns

number, gender, cases, articles

Romance nouns have gender. This noun has a typical masculine ending.

The accusative case becomes the basic form of singular nouns.

Plural number forms come from the nominative in Eastern Romance.

Romanian nouns still have genitive/dative and vocative case endings.

Plural number forms come from the accusative in Western Romance.

Classical Latin **lup-us**	
lupus	lupi
lupum	lupos
lupi	luporum
lupo	lupis
lupe	lupi
wolf	*wolves*

Romance languages use definite and indefinite articles with nouns.

Vulgar Latin ***lupu**
***illu lupu**
the wolf
***unu lupu**
a wolf

FEATURES

- Romance nouns tend to have two genders—masculine and feminine. Each noun is either masculine or feminine.

- Romance nouns have two numbers—singular (one instance) and plural (more than one).

- Romance nouns tend to have a single form for all cases, like when a noun is used as the subject versus as the object of a verb.

- Romance nouns are commonly paired with an article—indefinite (*an*), definite (*the*) or partitive (*some of*).

NOUN GENDERS

Latin initially classified nouns into three *genders*: masculine, feminine and neuter. As the language developed, masculine and neuter nouns mostly collapsed into a single masculine gender, while the feminine gender remained separate. In most modern Romance languages, nouns are either masculine or feminine. The issue of remaining "neuter" nouns is also worth some attention.

Masculine nouns

The languages show some correlation between the form of a noun and its gender. Classical Latin accusative case nouns ending in **-um** turned into Vulgar Latin nouns with **-u** after the noun's stem: Vulgar Latin *lacu *lake*. Although "**-u** nouns" included both masculine and neuter nouns in Vulgar Latin, later speakers began to treat most every noun ending in **-u** as *masculine* only.

The normal outcome of this masculine **-u** is the Romance noun ending **-o**, which still shows up today throughout Iberia and Italy (including Spanish, Portuguese and Italian): Vulgar Latin *lacu, Venetian **łago**, Italian **lago**, Spanish **lago** *lake*. Sardinian and Corsican speakers have a masculine **-u**, as do speakers of a number of South Italian languages and dialects: Sardinian **lagu**, Sicilian **lacu** *lake*.

In France, Switzerland, Eastern Spain, Romania and parts of Northern Italy, the masculine ending has worn away entirely. This <u>elision</u> may leave a final consonant as its signature. As a result, masculine nouns in Catalan, Occitan, French, Arpitan, Rhaeto-Romansh, Emiliano-Romagnolo and Romanian often end in a consonant: Catalan **llac**, Bolognese **lèg**, French **lac**, Romanian **lac** *lake*. One exception is the Aromanian language, closely related to Romanian, which retains the final **-u** where Romanian has lost it.

Romanian   **semn**   *sign*

Aromanian   **semnu** *sign*

The history of masculine **-o** in Spanish demonstrates the typical transformation of Latin **-um** into masculine **-o** in many languages.

Latin **murum** *wall* > *****muru** > Iberian *****muro** > Spanish **muro**

The development of masculine nouns ending in a consonant in Catalan shows how Latin **-um** disappeared entirely in languages like Occitan, Catalan, Romansh, French and Romanian.

Latin **murum** *wall* > *****muru** > Iberian *****muro** > Catalan **mur**

Latin nouns with an accusative ending **-em** or, rarely, a consonant are typically classified as masculine in the modern languages. In languages that preserve final vowels, like Italian and Sardinian, these nouns end in the vowel **-e**. In other languages, including French and Catalan, such nouns typically end in a consonant.

Vulgar Latin *****lacte** *milk* > Italian **latte** but French **lait**

This final example compares a single masculine noun, the word for *fact/deed*, across the Romance-speaking world. Notice which nouns have an equivalent of the masculine suffix **-u** or **-o**, and which have dropped the masculine ending.

Vulgar Latin	*factu
Portuguese	feito
Galician	feito
Old Spanish	fecho
Catalan	fet
Occitan	fach
French	fait
Franco-Provençal (Arpitan)	fét
Rhaeto-Romansh	fatg
Sardinian	fatu
Italian	fatto
Sicilian	fattu
Aromanian	faptu*
Romanian	fapt*

* Latin **factum** and its Romanian cognate **fapt(u)** are actually <u>neuter</u> in gender, though they resemble an <u>accusative</u> singular masculine noun.

Feminine nouns

As with masculine nouns, the form of a feminine noun sometimes gives away its gender. The <u>accusative case</u> of Classical Latin nouns ending in **-am** stands at the source of Vulgar Latin nouns with the ending **-a**. As Latin developed and split, most Romance _feminine_ nouns retained this final **-a**, weakened the <u>vowel</u> toward a neutral /ə/ (as in Portuguese, Catalan, Romanian and formal French) or deleted the vowel altogether (as in French).

In Iberian languages, Occitan, Franco-Provençal, Romansh, Italian and Romanian, the feminine ending is **-a** (Romanian **-ă**). Portuguese **casa**, Romanian **casă**, Romansh **chasa**, Italian **casa** for _house_ all have a stem **cas-** followed by the feminine ending.

The typical French feminine ending is "silent **-e**". Masculine nouns may end in a silent consonant, while nouns with the characteristically feminine "silent **-e**" retain their final consonant in pronunciation. This pattern leaves clear cases where the gender distinction is still explicit, although in a different way than most of Romance.

| French | **têt** | *small bowl* | /tɛ/ (with silent final t) |
| | **tête** | *head* | /tɛt/ (with silent final e) |

The modern languages also draw feminine nouns from Latin nouns with an accusative ending **-em**. In languages like Italian that retain final vowels, these feminines often end in **-e**. In other languages, including French and Catalan, these nouns may end in a consonant. For example, nouns with the endings **-itatem** *-ity*, **-tionem** *-tion* and **-sionem** *-sion* are feminine in Latin and in the modern languages.

*veritate *truth* > Sardinian **veridade**, Portuguese **verdade**, Italian **verità**

*solutione > Italian **soluzione**, Spanish **solución**, Catalan **solució**, Old Portuguese **soluçõ**

Some nouns in **-a** (French **-e**) are masculine, including those inherited from Greek neuter nouns in **-ma**: Spanish **problema**, French **problème** *problem*. This apparent exception does not apply to Romanian, where nouns like **problemă** have shifted to feminine.

Few ostensibly masculine nouns in **-o/-u** are feminine in gender. A notable exception in is the word for *hand*, which is feminine in nearly every Romance language: Vulgar Latin ***manu**, Asturian **manu**, French **main**, Sardinian **manu**, Italian **mano**. Romansh resolves this discrepancy by making **maun** masculine.

The table of examples below compares the outcome of one feminine noun, the word for *stone*, throughout Romance.

Vulgar Latin	*petra
Portuguese	pedra
Galician	pedra
Spanish	piedra
Catalan	pedra
Occitan	pèira
French	pierre
Franco-Provençal (Arpitan)	piérra
Sardinian	pedra
Italian	pietra
Neapolitan	preta
Sicilian	petra
Romanian	piatră

Neuter nouns

Latin neuter nouns were generally absorbed into the masculine gender as the modern languages developed.

Latin **centrum** > *centru *center* > Italian **centro**, Spanish **centro**, French **centre** (all masculine)

A few languages continue to distinguish a third gender. Most Vulgar Latin *neuters* resemble masculine nouns in the singular but feminine nouns in the plural: *centru *center*, *centra *centers*. A small set of nouns continues to abide by this pattern in Central Romance, including Standard Italian and Rhaeto-Romance. These nouns are usually masculine in the singular and plural, but have a "neuter" or "feminine" plural when they refer to a familiar pair or a collection. This usage, with apparently masculine forms in the singular and feminine in the plural, has been called the *indeterminate* or *collective neuter*.

Italian	**braccio** *arm,* **bracci** *arms,* **braccia** *pair of arms*
Romansh	**bratsch** *arm,* **bratschs** *arms,* **bratscha** *pair of arms*

*The Latin noun **Colosseum** (later **Coliseum**) is neuter, but modern forms like Italian **Colosseo** and French **Colisée** are masculine.*

Iberian languages like Asturian and Southern Italian languages like Neapolitan use a third gender for abstract nouns, collective nouns and other nouns. Such nouns are used in the singular, resemble masculine nouns and do not necessarily come from Latin neuters. In Neapolitan, the neuters differ from ordinary masculine nouns when the <u>definite article</u> is used. In Asturian, some of these nouns end in **-o** instead of the expected masculine **-u**.

Neapolitan	**'o latino** *the Latin man*	(masculine)
	'o llatino *the Latin language*	(neuter)
Asturian	**pelu** *[individual] hair*	(countable masculine noun)
	pelo *[bunch of] hair*	(non-countable neuter noun)

Romanian displays the most systematic use of a third gender, usually treated as neuter. Like Vulgar Latin, Romansh and Italian neuters just introduced, the Romanian neuter resembles the masculine in the singular and feminine in the plural.

Romanian   **timp** *time*, **centru** *center*   (both neuter)

The supplementary grammar tables at the end of this book contain examples of neuter nouns in relevant languages.

Determining noun gender

Determining the gender of a specific noun in a Romance language is not always a straightforward affair. In Catalan, Romansh, Occitan, Romanian and French, many endings have worn away or disappeared entirely. Still, certain patterns and common endings provide clues to noun gender beyond the typical masculine ***-u** and feminine ***-a** of singular nouns.

The gender of *cognates* remains reliably stable across all languages. For instance, given that Italian **cane** *dog* and Romanian **câine** *dog* are both masculine, the gender of French **chien** *dog* and Portuguese **cão** *dog* is, predictably, masculine. This kind of correspondence occurs between cognates derived from the same word in Latin.

Shared gender applies to cognates. It does not apply to words that have the same meaning but do not share an etymology: French **maison** *house* is not predictably feminine based on a comparison with Italian **casa** and Romanian **casă** *house*. Crucially, **maison** doesn't share a genetic relationship with those words. French **maison** comes from Vulgar Latin ***mansione**, while Romanian **casă** comes from a different word—the word ***casa**. French nouns in **-eur** serve as a major exception: Spanish **valor** and Italian **valore** are masculine, but French **valeur** is feminine.

Languages also have ways to form and modify nouns. Latin words formed by adding *derivational* endings. The Vulgar Latin endings ***-tione**, ***-sione** and ***-tate** are feminine in Latin and in all daughter languages: French **maison** comes from ***mansione**, a word with the characteristic feminine ending ***-sione**. Latin words ending in ***-tore**, ***-ismu** and ***-ma** are masculine in the modern languages. Word endings drive gender alignment—adding material (like prefixes) fails to sway a word's gender: Spanish **selección**, Romanian **selecție** *selection* and Spanish **preselección**, Romanian **preselecție** *preselection* are all feminine.

Productive derivational endings include *diminutives* (small or cherished nouns) and *augmentatives* (large, old or risible nouns): Spanish **casa** *house* versus **casita** *little house* and **casona** *old house*, Italian **ragazzo** *boy* versus **ragazzino** *little boy* and **ragazzaccio** *bad boy*. Languages often apply diminutives to other word classes, too: Catalan **bona** *good* but **bonica** *pretty* (an adjective), Portuguese **adeus** *farewell* versus **adeusinho** *bye-bye* (an interjection).

NOUN NUMBERS

Classical and Vulgar Latin nouns reflected two *numbers*—singular, for one instance of the noun, and plural, for two or more instances. This two-way distinction continues in the modern languages.

Singular nouns

The plain *singular* form of a Romance noun is its most basic, least marked form. Singulars tend to come from Vulgar Latin nouns ending in a vowel. The final vowels are ***-u**, nearly always masculine in gender, ***-a**, usually feminine in gender, and ***-e**, distributed among both genders.

In the modern languages, the typical masculine singular noun consists of a stem followed by **-o** (as in Spanish and Italian), **-u** (like Sardinian), or nothing but the stem where the Latin ***-u** has worn away entirely (as in French and Romanian). Typical feminine singulars have a stem plus **-a**, although this final vowel has weakened in languages like Catalan and French.

*muru *wall* > Italian **muro**, Romanian **mur** (masculine) *lingua *language* > Italian **lingua**, Romanian **limbă** (feminine)

Singular neuters of Southern Italy (Neapolitan) and Northern Spain (Asturian) act as mass nouns, uncountable nouns or abstract nouns: Asturian **pelu** *[strand of] hair* (masculine) contrasts with **pelo** *[bunch of] hair* (neuter). From another perspective, the masculine forms of these nouns are unmarked and the neuter nouns marked as abstract, which helps explain why the same stem may take both gender endings depending on its meaning.

The neuter nouns of Romanian, Italian and Rhaeto-Romansh are indistinguishable from masculine nouns in the singular: Romanian **braţ** *arm*, **un braţ** *an arm* (neuter) versus **român** *Romanian*, **un român** *a Romanian* (masculine).

Some Latin neuter plurals ending in **-a** were reinterpreted as feminine singulars by Vulgar Latin speakers. These words remain feminine singular in Romance: Latin **arma** *weapons* (neuter plural) becomes Spanish **arma**, French **arme** *weapon* (feminine singular).

Plural nouns

Romance languages mark singular nouns to form the *plural*. Languages fall into two camps: those that add a final **-s** to nouns to form the plural, and those that change the noun's final vowel to form the plural. Historically, this distinction depends on the Latin noun case used for the plural—nominative in Eastern Romance, accusative in Western Romance.

Portuguese, Spanish, French, Occitan, Sardinian and other Western Romance nouns build the plural by adding **-s** to the singular noun. Catalan spells the plural of feminine nouns in **-a** as **-es** rather than the expected **-as**: the plural of Catalan **casa** is **cases**.

Vulgar Latin *factu, *factos > Old Spanish **fecho**, **fechos** *fact, facts*

Vulgar Latin *casa, *casas > Spanish **casa**, **casas** *house, houses*

In Spain and Portugal, nouns ending in a consonant form the plural by adding **-es**: the plural of Spanish **hotel** is **hoteles**. French, Occitan, Catalan and Romansh add the plural **-s** directly to a final consonant: the plural of French **hôtel** is **hôtels**

In some cases, historical sound changes have obscured the pluralization process of an individual language. For example, the plural of Portuguese nouns ending in nasal vowels is not determinable from the ending alone: singular **situação** *situation* becomes plural **situações**, but singular **cão** *dog* becomes plural **cães**. The plurals are clearer when set alongside Vulgar Latin forms — ***situatione/*situationes** but ***cane/*canes**.

The plural **-s** has become silent in French, Franco-Provençal and some Occitan dialects. For many regular nouns, the singular and plural are written differently but sound identical. Speakers of these languages rely on other words, particularly the <u>articles</u>, to distinguish between singulars and plurals.

French   **clé**   *key*   (pronounced /kle/)
                  clés *keys*   (pronounced /kle/)

*The Venetian word **gondoła** has the plural **gondołe**, while the plural in Spanish is **góndolas**.*

Italian, Siclian, Dalmatian and other Eastern Romance nouns change the noun's final vowel to form the plural. Masculine nouns in *-u have a plural in *-i and feminine nouns in *-a form the plural with *-e. Singulars ending in *-e have a plural in *-i, whatever their gender: Italian **studente** *student* has the plural **studenti**.

| Italian | **fatto**, **fatti** | *fact, facts* |
| | **casa**, **case** | *house, houses* |

The neat Eastern pattern for pluralizing nouns is messier in Romanian. When a masculine singular noun ends in a consonant, the corresponding plural simply adds -i: **român** *Romanian* has the plural **români**. Feminine nouns ending in -ă change the vowel to -e or -i in the plural, depending on the noun: the plural of **casă** *house* is **case** but the plural of **lună** *moon* is **luni**. As in Italian, Romanian nouns ending in -e, often but not always masculine, have a plural in -i: masculine **câine** *dog* has the plural **câini**.

Romanian <u>neuters</u> tend to end in a consonant or -u in the singular. The corresponding plural adds -e or -uri to the final consonant, depending on the noun: the plural of **fapt** *fact* is **fapte** but the plural of **timp** *time* is **timpuri**. Romanian neuters ending in -u add -ri in the plural: **lucru** *thing* has the plural **lucruri**.

The <u>*collective neuter*</u> plurals of Romansh and Italian end in -a and contrast with regular masculine plurals. This plural ending is restricted to a small set of paired or grouped nouns.

| Italian | **braccio** *arm*, **bracci** *arms*, **braccia** *pair of arms* |
| Romansh | **bratsch** *arm*, **bratschs** *arms*, **bratscha** *pair of arms* |

Neapolitan and Asturian neuters act as mass nouns, uncountable nouns or abstract nouns: Asturian **pelo** has the collective meaning of *hair*. These nouns lack a plural form.

Noun Cases

Latin nouns had _case_ endings that linked the form of a noun to its role in a sentence. Vulgar Latin nouns began to combine cases and eventually lost case distinctions altogether.

In the modern languages, the Romance noun has a basic form derived from the Latin accusative singular. Languages add plural endings, which come from the Latin nominative plural in Eastern Romance and the accusative plural in Western Romance. Romanian also adds vocative and genitive/dative case endings to the basic form.

Accusative case

Latin _accusative_ nouns acted as the direct object of a verb and the object of many prepositions: compare **murus est...** [the] wall is... (nominative subject) to **construunt murum** [they] build [the] wall (accusative object). Vulgar Latin speakers began to use the accusative of the noun instead of other cases. In this way, the Latin accusative is the source of basic singular nouns in the modern language. The accusative origin of modern Romance nouns is clear when the nominative and accusative cases of the Latin noun differ markedly.

Latin **lingua** (nominative), **linguam** (accusative) > *lingua _language_ > Italian **lingua**, Spanish **lengua**

Latin **actio** (nominative), **actionem** (accusative) > *actione _action_ > Italian **azione**, Spanish **acción**

Unlike Romance pronouns, Romance nouns are not generally marked for case. Therefore, nouns derived from the Latin accusative are no longer limited to accusative use in the modern languages. For instance, Spanish **acción** can act as the subject of a verb, object of a verb or object of a preposition. The basic form of nouns in the modern languages works this way.

Not only does the basic singular form of Romance nouns come from the Latin accusative, but the accusative also gives Western

Romance its characteristic **-s** plural ending. The accusative plural of most Latin nouns (but not neuter nouns) contains this final **-s**.

*ventos *winds* (singular ***ventu**) > Spanish **vientos**, Catalan **vents**

*linguas *languages* (singular ***lingua**) > Spanish **lenguas**,
                                             Catalan **llengües**

*artes *arts* (singular ***arte**) > Spanish **artes**, Catalan **arts**

Neuter nouns in Latin generally fold into the masculine gender in the modern languages, which replace the neuter plural with the expected masculine accusative plural ***-os**: Latin **verbum** *word*, **verba** *words* > Spanish **verbo** *verb*, **verbos** *verbs*. Since Latin neuter nouns regularly have a nominative and accusative plural in ***-a**, the daughter languages have reanalyzed some neuter plurals as feminine singulars: Latin neuter plural **arma** *weapons* becomes feminine singular **arma** *weapon* in Spanish, Italian, Romansh and related languages.

In general, modern Romance nouns have the same form whether they act as subject or object, and that form comes from the Latin accusative. A few languages treat proper names and other personal nouns differently when they are the object of a verb, and this may be considered a modern *personal accusative*. For instance, Spanish insists on inserting the particle **a** before **Juan** in **veo a Juan** *I see John*, which marks **Juan** as the object. Romanian does the same with **pe** in **văd pe Ion** *I see John*.

Nominative case

Latin used the *nominative* case to mark the subject of a sentence or for nouns on either side of a copula: **Brutus construit...** *Brutus builds...*, **murus est** *[it] is [a] wall*. The nominative singular is also the canonical form of the noun cited in texts and dictionaries.

As explained in the previous section on accusatives, the role of the nominative began to diminish in Vulgar Latin. No modern language uses unique nominative case endings for nouns. The most significant contribution of the Latin nominative is seen in the Eastern

Romance plurals. While Western plurals derive from Latin <u>accusative</u> plurals in **-s**, Eastern plurals inherit the final vowels of the Latin nominative plural, which appear as masculine **-i** and feminine **-e** in Italian, Dalmatian and Romanian. Neapolitan and Sicilian reduce this plural to a single ending (Sicilian **-i**, Neapolitan **-e**).

*venti *winds* (singular ***ventu**) > Italian **venti**, Sicilian **venti**

*lingue *languages* (singular ***lingua**) > Italian **lingue**, Sicilian **lingui**

Eastern feminine plurals may instead derive from the accusative case: Vulgar Latin ***linguas** > Italian **lingue**. This fits with the fact that Latin plurals in **-es** now end in a vowel in Eastern Romance: ***artes** *arts* > Sicilian **arti**. Other instances of Latin words in **-s** becoming Eastern words with a final vowel also support an accusative derivation: ***adiutas** *you help* > Italian **aiuti**, Romanian **ajuți**.

Old French retained the distinction between nominative and accusative nouns, although the accusative case was extended to take on a more general oblique (non-nominative) role. This distinction shows up clearly when comparing the nominative and oblique forms of masculine nouns. Modern French has done away with this case system, again favoring the accusative as the source of the basic form and plural form of the French noun. The following table declines the masculine noun **loup** *wolf* in Late Latin and Old French.

	singular	plural
nominative	***lupus > loups**	***lupi > loup**
accusative	***lupu > loup**	***lupos > loups**

The Romance dismissal of the nominative singular has done away with the kind of variation found in "irregular" Latin noun paradigms. The asymmetry between irregular nominative singular forms of some Latin nouns alongside their regular non-nominative forms fails to carry over into the modern languages. For instance, the Latin nominative singular **nox** *night* has the stem **noct-** in all other cases (accusative singular **noctem**, accusative plural **noctes**). Since Romance languages do not draw their <u>cognates</u> from the nominative singular, they have regular patterns like Portuguese **noite**, **noites** and Italian **notte**, **notti** instead of Latin **nox**, **noctes** *night, nights*.

As mentioned, modern Romance nouns have the same form whether acting as subject or object, and that form derives from the Latin accusative. A few languages treat <u>proper names</u> differently: Spanish **Juan** is the nominative subject in **Juan espera** *John waits* but **a Juan** is the accusative object in **veo a Juan** *I see John*. Similarly, Catalan uses masculine **en** or feminine **na** to mark a proper noun acting as a subject but the regular <u>definite article</u> with a proper noun as object: **en Joan espera** *John waits* but **veig el Joan** *I see John*. Although distinct from the Latin case system, these grammatical structures still productively distinguish between nominative and accusative case.

The **Ponte Vecchio** *("Old Bridge")* in Florence. Latin nominative
pons had an accusative **pontem**. Modern Romance words for
"bridge" derive from that accusative form.

Genitive & other cases

The Romance languages do not generally retain noun endings from cases beyond the accusative and nominative. The sections above describe the remnants of Latin noun cases in most modern languages. The visible exception is Romanian, which has the basic singular and plural noun forms described above as well as a secondary case derived from the Latin _genitive_ (possessive).

Romanian nouns have the basic form described above when the noun is the subject of a verb, the object of a verb or the object of a preposition. However, nouns take a genitive/dative case ending when the noun is a possessor or recipient. The genitive/dative may appear on the bare noun: **persoană** _person_ (base), **persoane** _person_ (genitive/dative). However, the genitive is normally marked with an indefinite or definite <u>article</u>: **persoanei** _to/for the person_, **persoanelor** _to/for the persons_.

Vulgar Latin ***persona** _person_ > Romanian **persoană**

Vulgar Latin ***persone** _person's_ > Romanian **persoane**

Like English, the Romance languages tend to distinguish grammatical cases through word order (especially nominative versus accusative) and with prepositions (like the possessive and the dative): **di Anna** _Anna's_. Even Romanian, with its inherited genitive case, makes strong use of word order and analytic constructions where Latin case endings once sufficed: **de oameni** _of people_, **lui Ion** _to John_ (literally _to-him John_).

case	Latin endings	Spanish prepositions	
accusative	**Romam**	**a Roma**	_to Rome_ (motion)
genitive	**Romae**	**de Roma**	_of Rome / Rome's_
dative	**Roma**	**para Roma**	_to/for Rome_ (recipient)
locative	**Romae**	**en Roma**	_in Rome_

In comparison, the Romance <u>pronouns</u> do preserve formal cases.

Vocative case

A _vocative_ noun form, used for calling out the noun, persists in Romanian. The Romanian vocative is substantially different from the

Latin vocative in form. Masculine and neuter singular nouns ending in a consonant add **-e** or **-ule** to form the vocative (**-ul** is the masculine definite article in Romanian). Feminine singular nouns in **-ă** have a vocative in **-o**. Plural nouns end in **-lor**, which is also the genitive plural definite article.

Romanian   **Nicu** *Nick*, **Nicule!** *Nick!*
             Ană *Anna*, **Ano!** *Anna!*

While not a separate formal case, the term vocative also applies to a bare noun in languages that would otherwise use an <u>article</u> with the noun: Catalan **en Pere és...** *Peter is...* but **Pere!** *Peter!*

ARTICLES

Although *articles* did not occur with nouns in Classical Latin, speakers of Vulgar Latin began to use demonstrative adjectives for the definite article *the* and the numeral *one* for the indefinite article *an*. All modern Romance languages inherit both definite and indefinite articles, which follow the number, gender and case pattern of <u>nouns</u>. Languages differ as to how they use a noun with no article and whether they have developed a further partitive article.

Definite articles

All branches of Romance have developed <u>*definite articles*</u> that specify nouns, even though early Latin had none. The modern definite article typically comes from Vulgar Latin ***illu** for masculine nouns and ***illa** for feminine nouns, both accusative singular forms of the same Latin pronoun **ille** *that*: ***illu dictu** *that saying* acquired the meaning *the saying* and ***illa casa** *that house* came to mean *the house*.

***illu factu** *the fact* (masculine) > Italian **il fatto**, Portuguese **o feito**,
French **le fait**

*illa lingua *the language* (feminine) > Italian **la lingua**, Portuguese **a língua**, French **la langue**

The reliance on the accusative singular parallels the development of Romance nouns from Latin <u>noun cases</u>. In the same way, the plural definite article draws on the nominative plural of **ille** in Eastern Romance but the accusative plural in Western Romance. Languages that source their noun plurals from the Latin accusative plural have definite articles with the same plural ending, while languages that rely on the nominative plural also do so for the definite article.

*illi facti *the facts* (nominative) > Italian **i fatti**, Sicilian **li fatti**

*illos factos (accusative) > Old Spanish **los fechos**, Portuguese **os feitos**, French **les faits**

The accusative forms of Latin **ipse** *self/same* provided another source for definite articles. Few modern languages opt for this article—its use is mainly confined to the Balearic Islands and Sardinia. Indeed, one characteristic feature of Balearic Catalan and Sardinian is the distinctive **s**-article instead of the **l**-article of mainland Romance.

*issu factu *the fact* > Balearic **es fet**, Sardinian **su fatu**

*issa lingua *the language* > Balearic **sa llengua**, Sardinian **sa limba**

*issas linguas *the languages* > Balearic **ses llengües**, Sardinian **sas limbas**

Some languages employ a <u>neuter</u> definite article. Spanish uses the article **lo** instead of the expected **el** to turn a masculine adjective into a noun: **lo rojo** *the red [thing]*. Although the Neapolitan neuter article **'o** is the same as the masculine **'o**, neuter nouns often double their initial consonant after the neuter article: **'o napulitano** *the Neapolitan [man]* versus **'o nnapulitano** *the Neapolitan [language]*.

Italian, Swiss, French and Eastern Iberian languages eagerly allow contraction when the article precedes a word beginning in a vowel: French l'amie *the [female] friend* instead of *la amie, Catalan l'amic *the [male] friend*, Rhaeto-Romansh l'amia *the [female] friend* rather than *la amia, Sardinian s'amicu *the [male] friend*.

All forms of the definite article have undergone radical changes in Western Iberian languages like Portuguese and Galician. The intervocalic -l- of ille disappears and the resulting contraction produces the definite articles o, a, os and as. Compare Portuguese o amigo *the [male] friend* and a amiga *the [female] friend* to Spanish el amigo and la amiga.

The placement of the definite article is fairly uniform across all languages. It stands as a distinct word to the left of the noun: Spanish la idea *the idea*. The article also remains to the left of any modifying words, which may fall between the article and the noun: la buena idea *the good idea*. The notable exception to this trend is Romanian, which attaches the definite article to the end of the noun.

Romanian masculine and neuter singular nouns add the definite article -ul: român *Romanian* becomes românul *the Romanian*. Masculine and neuter nouns ending in -e add -le instead: nume *name*, numele *the name*. Feminine nouns in -ă replace the final vowel with a strong -a: persoană *person*, persoana *the person*. In the plural, masculine nouns add an -i: români *Romanians*, românii *the Romanians*. Feminine and neuter plurals attach -le: persoane *persons*, persoanele *the persons*. All of these endings come from forms of Latin ille.

Romanian nouns also have a genitive/dative ending, and the articles reflect that case. The <u>genitive</u> definite article on masculine and neuter nouns is -(u)lui: românului *to/for the Romanian*, numelui *to/for the name*. Feminine nouns attach a definite article -i to the genitive form, which always resembles the feminine plural: persoanei *to/for the person*. In the plural, the genitive article for all nouns is -lor: românilor *to/for the Romanians*, persoanelor *to/for the persons*.

This next table displays the forms of a masculine noun in Romanian both with and without the definite article.

Vulgar Latin	Romanian	
*romanu	român	*Romanian*
*romanu illu	românul	*the Romanian*
*romanu illui	românului	*to/for the Romanian*
*romani	români	*Romanians*
*romani illi	românii	*the Romanians*
*romani illoru	românilor	*to/for the Romanians*

Proper nouns (names of people and places) are found without an article: Spanish **a Juan** *to John*, Romanian **România este o țară** *Romania is a country*, French **Jeanne parle néerlandais** *Jane speaks Dutch*. Names of countries routinely take the definite article in some languages: Portuguese **para a Itália** *to Italy* (literally *to the Italy*), French **la France** *France*. Some languages allow definite articles with names: Catalan **en Pere parla**, Portuguese **o Pedro fala** but not French ***le Pierre parle** for *Peter speaks*.

*This cathedral in Palma is known as **sa Seu** in Balearic Catalan (with the feminine definite article *****issa***) but **la Seu** on the continent (with the definite article *****illa***).*

In many Romance languages the definite articles contract with certain <u>prepositions</u>, most notably **de** *of*: Italian **dell'idea** *of the idea*, (**de** + **la**), Spanish **del hombre** *of the man* (**de** + **el**), French **des chansons** *of the songs* (**de** + **les**), Portuguese **das línguas** *of the languages* (**de** + **as**), Galician **pola xente** *by the people* (**por** + **a**).

Indefinite articles

The general use and history of the Romance <u>*indefinite article*</u> is straightforward. The singular indefinite article is universally based on Vulgar Latin ***unu**/***una**, which are the masculine and feminine <u>accusative</u> forms of **unus** *one*.

***unu factu** *a fact* > Portuguese **um feito**, Romanian **un fapt**,
Italian **un fatto**, Sardinian **unu fatu**

***una lingua** *a language* > Portuguese **uma língua**, Romanian **o limbă**,
Italian **una lingua**, Sardinian **una limba**

The masculine singular indefinite is generally shortened from ***unu** to ***un** in the modern languages: Portuguese **um homem**, Occitan **un òme**, Romansh **in um**, Italian **un uomo**, Romanian **un om** for *a man*. This same shortening trend does not apply to the feminine indefinite article: Portuguese **uma casa**, Occitan **una casa**, Romansh **ina chasa**, Italian **una casa**, Romanian **o casă** all translate to *a house*. French shortens both articles to a single syllable: masculine **un** /œ̃/, which drops final **-n** and nasalizes the vowel, and **une** /yn/, where the final **-e** is silent.

Italian languages may contract the feminine indefinite article when the following word begins with a vowel: Italian **un'idea** for **una idea** *an idea*.

Romanian has an additional <u>dative/genitive case</u>. With the <u>definite article</u>, this case appears as distinct noun endings: **român** *Romanian*, **românul** *the Romanian*, **românului** *to/for the Romanian*. When a genitive case construction involves an indefinite article instead, the indefinite article marks the case: **unui român** *to/for a Romanian*, **unor român** *to/for some Romanians*. The masculine and neuter genitive indefinite is **unui**, the feminine is **unei** and the plural is **unor** for all genders.

Romance languages shy away from plural indefinite articles (formed from the plural of *one*), although they do have currency in Iberia: Galician **unhas linguas** *some languages*, Portuguese **uns feitos** *some facts*, Spanish **unos dichos** *some sayings*. One avoidance strategy found throughout the Romance world explicitly employs the word for *some*: Spanish **algunas casas**, Italian **alcune case**, and Romanian **niște case** all mean *some houses*.

However, languages commonly use a partitive article or no article whatsoever to give a plural noun an indefinite meaning. These two article types are the focus of the next section.

Zero articles & partitive articles

Most of the Romance languages allow singular nouns to ditch the article in certain cases. This _zero article_ (lack of an article) may occur when a singular noun is used in a non-specific way: Spanish **ella tomó vino** *she drank wine*, **es mala idea** *it's a bad idea* (literally *it's bad idea*). The zero article is not always found where English allows it, such as with singular abstract nouns: French **la géographie** *geography* (literally *the geography*), Romanian **creştinismul este o religie** *Christianity is a religion* (literally *the Christianity*), Italian **la giustizia** *justice* (literally *the justice*), Aragonese **o estudio d'o lenguache** *the study of language* (literally *the study of the language*).

Italian and French build a singular and plural _partitive_ out of Vulgar Latin ***de*** *of* plus the _definite article_ ***illu***. The resulting construction has the meaning *some (of the)* and is used for indeterminate quantities: French **du vin**, Italian **del vino** *some wine* (a quantity of wine) versus **le vin**, **il vino** *wine* (general concept of wine or specific wine). This partitive covers situations where other languages use a noun with no article: French **il boit du vin** *he drinks some wine* versus Portuguese **bebe vinho** *[he] drinks wine*, which achieves the same meaning without an article. French, in particular, avoids nouns without an indefinite, definite or partitive article: Asturian has **ye vinu** *[it] is wine* but French needs **c'est du vin** *it's some* *wine*, **c'est un vin** *it's a wine* or **c'est le vin** *it's the wine*, not the bare *c'est vin.

Plural nouns with an indefinite meaning often occur with the word for *some*: Spanish **algunas ideas** *some ideas*. Italian and French may use the plural partitive in these cases: Italian **delle lingue**, French **des langues** for *some languages*. Most languages, including Spanish, Italian and Romanian, can simply drop the article altogether in the plural: compare Spanish **aprender lenguas** *learn languages* to French **apprendre des langues** *learn (some) languages* and **apprendre les langues** *learn the languages*.

Verbs

person & number, tense & aspect, mood, helping verbs

Romance verbs have <u>non-finite</u> forms like this fourth <u>conjugation</u> infinitive.

Romance verb endings still reflect the <u>person</u> and <u>number</u> of the subject.

Classical Latin **ven-ire**

venio	*I come*	**venimus**	*we come*
venis	*you come*	**venitis**	*you all come*
venit	*(s)he comes*	**veniunt**	*they come*

Verb endings change to indicate different <u>tenses</u> and <u>moods</u>. These are present tense, indicative mood endings.

<u>Perfects</u> and <u>passives</u> use the helping verbs ***abere** and ***essere**.

Vulgar Latin ***venire**

*abent/sunt venitu
they have come
*stant veniendu
they are coming

Romance languages use a number of <u>auxiliary verbs</u> in common constructions.

FEATURES

Verb endings:

- Romance verbs change to indicate <u>person</u> and <u>number</u>—the distance of removal from the speaker (first, second, third person) and whether the action is performed by one person (singular) or more than one (plural). <u>Non-finite</u> forms of the verb fail to reflect person and number.

- Romance verbs reflect multiple <u>tenses</u>, which are actually tense/aspect combinations—an action started now or very soon (present), a one-time action in the past (preterit), an ongoing action in the past (imperfect) or an action yet to be performed (future).

- Romance verbs use <u>moods</u> to express a variety of attitudes toward the action—a mood for making a statement or asking a question (indicative), issuing a command (imperative), stating a desired or contrary-to-fact action (subjunctive) or saying what would be the case (conditional).

Auxiliaries & Analytic Constructions:

- Romance verbs use the auxiliaries *have* and *be* to form <u>perfects</u> and <u>passives</u>—an action is done (passive) or someone has done an action (perfect).

- Romance verbs require the assistance of <u>helping verbs</u> in a number of constructions—*is doing* (present progressive), *going to do* (near future), *can* or *should do* (modal auxiliaries), *prefer to do* (phrasal verbs) and so on.

PERSON & NUMBER

Latin verbs have a stem followed by a grammatical ending that contains information about the agent, specifically the <u>person and number</u> of the subject. This way of building verbs continues into the modern languages. The examples below will stick to the present <u>tense</u> and the indicative <u>mood</u>, since these are basic and uniform throughout Romance.

Persons

Latin and the Romance languages count three _persons_ from the perspective of the speaker. The speaker is _I_ (the first person), the addressee is _you_ (the second person), and a person removed from the conversation is _he/she/it_ (the third person). This discussion will concentrate on the verb forms used for these persons rather than the subject pronouns themselves, but verbs and pronouns do intertwine in the grammar.

Latin and Romance verbs take different endings to mark these three persons: Italian **parlo** _I speak_ (first person), **parli** _you speak_ (second person), **parla** _he/she speaks_ (third person). Although Romance, like English, has multiple third-person pronouns, verbs have a single third-person ending: Catalan **ell parla** _he speaks_, **ella parla** _she speaks_.

Verb endings reflect the person performing the action, and Latin and most of the modern languages tend to drop the subject pronoun: Latin **facio**, Italian **faccio**, Portuguese **faço**, Romanian **fac** all mean _I make_. Romansh, French and some Northern Italian languages have abandoned this _pro-drop_ feature. These languages do not drop subject pronouns: Romansh **jau tschertg** _I search_ but not just *****tschertg**, Emiliano-Romagnolo **a cerc** _I search_ but not *****cerc** alone, French **je cherche** but not *****cherche** for _I search_.

Languages vary when it comes to the degree of difference between person endings. In Spanish, Portuguese and Italian, verbs clearly distinguish first, second and third person. In the extreme case, French endings have worn away so much that the first, second and third person have the same pronunciation, even when spelled differently: the verb in French **je trouve** _I find_, **tu trouves** _you find_ and **il/elle trouve** _he/she finds_ is pronounced /truv/ for all three persons.

The third person singular is used for masculine or feminine singular nouns and pronouns: French **la femme parle** _the woman speaks_, **il parle** _he speaks_. The third person also agrees with neuter pronouns in languages that have them: Portuguese **isso basta**, French **ça suffit**, Occitan **açò basta** for _it/that suffices_.

The third person offers a _formal_ way to address _you_ throughout the Romance-speaking world, perhaps under the notion that speaking to someone indirectly suggests a higher level of respect. This development postdates Latin but has wide currency: Galician **vostede fala** *you (formal) speak* (grammatical third person) versus familiar **tu falas** (grammatical second person), Italian **Lei parla** (third person) *you (formal) speak* against the informal **tu parli** (second person). Languages can still drop these formal pronouns: Galician **fala galego** *you (formal) speak Galician* or *he/she speaks Galician* (depending on context). French does not participate in this development, and instead employs the second-person plural for this purpose.

French and Romansh have a singular <u>indefinite pronoun</u> that parallels the use of English *one does, we do* or the generic *you do* (as when giving instructions). This pronoun occurs with third-person verb endings: French **on dit** *one says / we say*, Romansh **ins lavura** *one works*. French speakers now prefer this pronoun and the related third-person verb for expressing *we* in conversation: **on parle français** *we speak French*. Catalan and Occitan have related pronouns, but these are not as pervasive.

The following table abstracts first, second and third person endings based on their degree of fidelity or closeness to the Latin endings. Early Latin built verb endings with a <u>thematic vowel</u> (**a/e/i**) plus a person marker (**o/s/t**). Languages like Sardinian and Spanish fall closer to the Latin endings, while languages like French fall to the far right.

	Early endings	Latin endings	Romance endings	Weak Romance endings
1st person	vowel+o	**-o/-eo/-io**	**-o**	**-e/-i**
2nd person	vowel+s	**-as/-es/-is**	**-as/-es**	**-e(s)/-i(s)**
3rd person	vowel+t	**-at/-et/-it**	**-a/-e**	**-e/-i**

The next table compares the first, second and third singular forms of **amare** *to love* in representative languages.

Latin	Sardinian	Spanish	Italian	Catalan	French	
amao/amo	**amo**	**amo**	**amo**	**amo**	**aime**	*I love*
amas	**amas**	**amas**	**ami**	**ames**	**aimes**	*you love*
amat	**amat**	**ama**	**ama**	**ama**	**aime**	*she/he loves*

Numbers

The previous section presented singular verb forms for the first, second and third person. Latin and Romance verbs have a corresponding plural _number_ for all three persons: Vulgar Latin ***fabulas** _you speak_ differs from ***fabulatis** _all of you speak_, and French **il travaille** _he works_ contrasts with **ils travaillent** _they work_.

The first-person plural matches the pronoun _we_, the second-person plural is _all of you_ and the third plural is _they_. Romance pronouns do distinguish gender in the third-person plural, unlike their English counterparts: Romanian **ei lucrează**, Catalan **ells treballen** _they work_ (masculine or mixed-gender group) versus Romanian **ele lucrează**, Catalan **elles treballen** _they (all feminine) work_. Notice that the verb endings do not change based on the gender.

The practice of dropping subject pronouns (_pro-drop_) is equally exercised in the plural: Vulgar Latin ***fabulamus**, Portuguese **falamos** _we speak_ alongside **nós falamos** _we (emphatic) speak_. Again, some languages no longer drop the subject: French has **ils parlent** _they speak_ but not just ***parlent**.

As mentioned above, conversational French uses the pronoun **on** with a third-person singular verb where written French has **nous** _we_ with a first-person plural ending: colloquial **on parle latin** exists alongside the formal **nous parlons latin** for _we speak Latin_. Speakers of Rhaeto-Romansh, Occitan and Catalan have access to a similar pronoun.

The second-person plural also provides a courteous, _formal_ way of addressing one person (_you, sir or madam_) in French, Romansh and Romanian: Romansh **Vus vegnis**, French **vous venez**, Romanian **(dumneavoastră) veniți** all translate to _you (polite) come_. Among these languages, Romanian often drops the subject. Although the Iberian languages avoid this application of the second plural, a similar use is found in traditional religious contexts: Spanish **Vos sois el Señor** _Thou art the Lord_.

Just as with the third-person singular, third-person plural forms are used to address a group politely throughout the Romance-speaking world: Italian **Loro parlano** and Galician **vostedes falan** are polite ways of saying _all of you speak_. In Portuguese and Latin

American Spanish, the second plural has been replaced by third-person plural forms, which are now used exclusively for plural address: Spanish **ustedes hablan**, Portuguese **vocês falam** for *all of you speak* (third plural) where a Spaniard might have **vosotros habláis** (second plural). French, Romansh and some other languages do not share this use of the third-person plural.

*A Parisian tour bus invites sightseers aboard with the second-person plural form of the verb **découvrir** ("to discover").*

Many dialects of Latin American Spanish now use a form derived from the second-person plural for singular address: **vos hablás** alongside **tú hablas** for *you (singular) speak*, although the difference can be a social marker.

As with the singular, languages vary when it comes to the degree of difference between endings. In Sardinian, Iberian and Italian, verbs clearly distinguish between the singular and plural of all persons. On the other hand, French verbs do not clearly distinguish between the singular and plural, especially when it comes to the third person: the verb in **il trouve** *he finds* and **ils trouvent** *they find* is pronounced /truv/ in both numbers. Similarly, the third-person plural ending in Romanian always coincides either with the third-person singular or the first-person singular form of the verb: **eu fac** *I do,* **ei fac** *they do* versus **ea face** *she does.*

Early Latin built plural verb endings with a <u>thematic vowel</u> (**a/e/i**) plus a person marker (**mus/tis/nt**). This next table compares the person-number endings that get added to regular Latin verbs in the <u>present tense</u>.

	singular	example	plural	example
1st person	-o	amo	-mus	amamus
2nd person	-s	amas	-tis	amatis
3rd person	-t	amat	-nt	amant

The following table compares the plural endings of a regular verb across representative languages.

Latin	Sardinian	Spanish	Italian	Catalan	French	
amamus	amamus	amamos	amiamo	amem	aimons	*we love*
amatis	amades	amáis	amate	ameu	aimez	*you all love*
amant	aman(t)	aman	amano	amen	aiment	*they love*

TENSE

Latin verb endings carry information about the time of an action (*tense*) as well as the duration of an action (*aspect*). The modern languages inherit this robust verb system, although all languages have simplified the Latin endings to some degree. The examples below assume familiarity with <u>person</u> and <u>number</u>. Romance verb forms are normally classed according to their tense-aspect and their <u>mood</u>. The mood will be held constant these examples—only the basic indicative mood will be used in order to draw attention to the verb's tenses.

Stems, thematic vowels & conjugations

Latin verbs build their endings out of multiple parts. The first component is the verb's <u>stem,</u> which is the part that carries its meaning: Vulgar Latin ***parabol-asti** *you talked* has a stem ***parabol-**

talk and an ending **-asti** that gives grammatical information about the verb. When the verb stem changes, the meaning of the verb changes: ***parabol-asti** *you spoke* but ***cant-asti** *you sang*. When the verb endings change, it is the grammatical use of the verb that changes: ***parabol-as** *you talk*, ***parabol-asti** *you talked*, ***parabol-ai** *I talked*. Unlike English verb stems, which often have no endings, Latin and Romance stems are abstract units that require grammatical endings when they are used in actual speech: Vulgar Latin ***tu parabol-as** but not just ***tu parabol-** for *you speak*.

The next important component is the _thematic vowel_, which allows verbs to be classified according to the vowel found after the verb stem. Every Latin verb has one of four possible thematic vowels: the vowel **a**, the vowel **e**, the vowel **i** and a zero vowel or unstressed vowel **ĕ**. The rest of the verb endings follow this vowel: Vulgar Latin ***parabolare** *to speak* has a stem ***parabol-** and a thematic vowel **-a-**, while ***finire** *to finish* has a stem ***fin-** and a thematic **-i-**. Important contrasts and similarities between the verbs appear once tense endings are applied: ***parabol-a-s** *you speak* has a thematic vowel **-a-** and a second-person singular **-s**, while ***fin-i-s** *you finish* has a thematic **-i-** but the same second-person singular ending **-s**.

Vulgar Latin verbs may be cited by their infinitives, since these relate to no specific person or number but still show the thematic vowel of the verb. Verbs with thematic **-a-** have an infinitive **-are** and belong to the first conjugation (I). Verbs with the thematic vowel **-e-** have an infinitive **-ere** and belong to the second conjugation (II). Verbs with the unstressed vowel **-ĕ-** and infinitive **-ĕre** form the third conjugation (III). Finally, verbs with thematic **-i-** and an infinitive **-ire** fall in the fourth conjugation (IV).

First conjugation	Second conjugation	Third conjugation	Fourth conjugation
-are	**-ere**	**-ĕre**	**-ire**

The four-way distinction between Latin _conjugations_ survives in Italian and, to some extent, in French, Catalan, Occitan, Romanian and Romansh. Iberian languages merged the awkward conjugation III into IV or II, depending on the verb and the language: ***vincĕre** *to win* becomes Spanish **vencer** (II) and Portuguese **vencer** (II), but ***dicĕre** *to* *say* turns into Spanish **decir** (IV) and Portuguese **dizer** (II). Sardinian conflates conjugations II and III, shuffling **-ere** verbs into the unstressed **-ĕre** conjugation: Vulgar Latin ***potere** *to be able* becomes Sardinian **pòdere**. Conjugations II and III come to look more alike in all languages, tending towards thematic **-e-**.

	First conjugation	Second conjugation	Third conjugation	Fourth conjugation
Latin	**-are**	**-ere**	**-ĕre**	**-ire**
Italian	**-are**	**-ere**	**-ĕre**	**-ire**
Sardinian	**-are**	**-ĕre**	**-ĕre**	**-ire**
Catalan	**-ar**	**-er**	**-re**	**-ir**
French	**-er**	**-oir**	**-re**	**-ir**
Romansh	**-ar**	**-air**	**-er**	**-ir**
Romanian	**-a**	**-ea**	**-e**	**-i**
Spanish	**-ar**	**-er/-ir**	**-er/-ir**	**-ir**
Portuguese	**-ar**	**-er/-ir**	**-er/-ir**	**-ir**

The first conjugation (in ***-are**) often gets labelled "open" or "productive". This conjugation is the main source of new verbs derived from a variety of word classes (often nouns): from a noun stem **telefon-** *telephone* come Catalan **telefonar**, French **téléphoner**, Romanian **telefona** *to phone / to call*.

The class or conjugation of a Romance verb is easily determined from its infinitive. This guide follows the lead of many reference materials and instructors in referring to verb conjugations by their associated infinitive, such as "French **-er** verbs" instead of "French verbs that descend from a Latin verb with a thematic vowel **a**".

Present tense

The *present tense* is used for ongoing and habitual actions in the present: Romanian **lucrez** means *I work* or *I am working*. In addition, the Romance present marks an action that will happen soon: Spanish **mañana trabajo** *I am working / will work tomorrow*. All Romance languages inherit the Latin present tense for this purpose, which is built from a verb stem, a thematic vowel and present-tense endings: Latin *fabul-a-s, Old Spanish **fablas** *you speak*. The six present endings for each verb correspond to the six person-number combinations.

In Central and Eastern Romance, including Occitan, Catalan, French, Italian, Romanian and Romansh, some **–ire** verbs take an augment between the verb stem and the ending: Italian **finire** *to finish* has forms like **finisco** *I finish* and **finiscono** *they finish* rather than *fino and *finono. A number of common **-ir** verbs do not take the augment in these languages: Italian **dorme** (**dormire**), Romanian **doarme** (**dormi**) for *he sleeps* (*to sleep*). Rhaeto-Romansh adds this augment to the present indicative of many **-ar** verbs as well: **ins sperescha** (**sperar**) for *one hopes* (*to hope*).

All languages have "irregular" verbs in the present, especially when it comes to **-ere**, **-ĕre** and **-ire** verbs. Irregular present forms often preserve a Latin feature lost in the formation of regular verbs: Latin *venio *I come* becomes Portuguese **venho**, Italian **vengo**, Sardinian **venzo** rather than the expected *veno.

Many languages have altered the pronunciation of stressed vowels **o** and **e** within the verb stem. This results in a set of *stem-changing* verbs, in which the singular and third-person plural stems have one vowel (often a diphthong), but first plural and second plural stems have a different vowel: Spanish **pierdes** *you lose* versus **perdemos** *we lose* and **perder** *to lose*, or Italian **vuole** *he wants* versus **volete** *all of you want* and the infinitive **volere**. Verbs with similar stem changes in Portuguese, Spanish, Catalan, Occitan, French and Italian include *morire *to die* and *potere *to be able*. Such radical-changing verbs are particularly prevalent in Ibero-Romance.

The verb tables at the end of this book include a comparison of verbs in the present tense in many Romance languages.

Preterit (simple past)

The Latin verb can also take a set of endings for single events that were completed in the past. In Classical Latin, this historic past or *preterit* is constructed by adding a thematic vowel, **-v-**, and the tense ending to the verb's stem: **am-a-v-i** *I loved*, **fin-i-v-imus** *we finished* and so on. Vulgar Latin prefers shorter endings, which begin to resemble the past tense forms in the modern languages: Vulgar Latin **am-a-i** *I loved*, **fin-i-mus** *we finished* and the like.

fabul-a-sti *you spoke* > Portuguese **falaste**, Asturian **falasti**,
Old Spanish **fablaste**

parabol-a-i *I spoke* > Catalan **parlí**, French **parlai**, Italian **parlai**

parabol-a-runt *they spoke* > French **parlèrent**, Occitan **parlèron**,
Italian **parlarono**

The preterit presents many irregular or unexpected forms, especially from **-ĕre** verbs. A number of Latin verbs have unique past stems, including stems that insert **-s-** before the ending or change a vowel. These irregular verbs include basic vocabulary items like **dic-ĕre** *to say* and **fac-ĕre** *to do*.

Latin **dic-s-i** *I said* > Italian **dissi**, Portuguese **disse**, Romanian **zisei**

Latin **inclu-s-i** *I included* > Italian **inclusi**, French **inclus**,
Romanian **inclusei**

Latin **fec-i** *I did* > Italian **feci**, Portuguese **fiz**, French **fis**

Latin **fu-erunt** *they were* > Italian **furono**, Spanish **fueron**,
French **furent**, Romanian **fură**

In most of Central and Eastern Romance, this simple past is relegated to literary use: French **je parlai** *I spoke* appears in print but not in conversation, where **j'ai parlé** (literally *I have spoken*) is heard instead. French, Romansh, Standard Italian, Romanian (but not Aromanian) and Sardinian all limit themselves to this kind of <u>perfect</u> construction (similar to English *they have done*) to talk about one-time events in the past.

The verb tables at the end of this book compare verbs in the preterit across many Romance languages.

Imperfect (ongoing past)

Latin verb endings can also refer to a continuous or habitual past action. The Latin _imperfect_ is formed with a verb stem, the thematic vowel, an imperfect marker **-ba-** and a series of endings similar to the present tense suffixes: ***am-a-ba-s** _you used to love / were loving_, ***fin-i-ba-s** _you were finishing / used to finish_. Although often called a tense, the imperfect differs from the simple past in its _aspect_: imperfect endings mark an ongoing action, while the preterit indicates a one-time event.

Vulgar Latin ***cantabant in latinu** _they were singing in Latin_ > Italian **cantavano in latino**, Spanish **cantaban en latín**

Vulgar Latin ***cantarunt in latinu** _they sang in Latin_ > Italian **cantarono in latino**, Spanish **cantaron en latín**

Many languages preserve the lengthy Latin imperfect quite faithfully, often changing **-b-** to **-v-**: Italian **amava**, Portuguese **amava**, Asturian **amaba** mean _(s)he used to love_. Some languages do away with the middle **-b-** entirely: Romanian **credea**, Medieval Italian **credea** versus Modern Italian **credeva** for _he used to believe_.

Languages without medial **-b-** typically have a sequence of vowels beginning in **-i-** or **-ai-**: Sardinian **tue amaias** (**amare**), French **tu aimais** (**aimer**) for _you were loving_ (_to love_). Iberian languages (including Catalan and Occitan) cut both ways, keeping **-b-** in **-ar** verbs but dropping it in **-er** and **-ir** verbs: Vulgar Latin ***fabl-a-b-amus** alongside Portuguese **falávamos** _we used to speak_, but ***part-i-b-amus** versus Portuguese **partíamos** _we used to depart_.

*tenebat _he was holding_ > Italian **teneva**, Romansh **teneva**, Romanian **ținea**, Sardinian **tenìat**, French **il tenait**, Spanish **tenía**

*teneba _I was holding_ > Italian **tenevo**, Romansh **teneva**, Romanian **țineam**, Sardinian **tenìo**, French **je tenais**, Spanish **tenía**

Imperfect verbs are often used alongside simple past tense verbs. In particular, the imperfect can be used to narrate background events which are interrupted by simple past actions: Italian **ascoltava musica quando telefonai**, Portuguese **escutava música quando telefonei** *he was listening (imperfect) to music when I called (simple past)*.

Unlike the Romance preterit, the imperfect is relatively free of irregularities. The Romance verb tables at the end of this book compare verbs in the imperfect across many languages at once.

The **Padrão dos Descobrimentos** *("Monument of the Discoveries") in Lisbon. The Portuguese verb* **explorar** *has preterit forms like* **exploraram** *("they explored") and imperfect forms like* **exploravam** *("they used to explore").*

Future tense

Many Romance languages use a set of verb endings to mark that an action will take place in the future. Latin originally formed the *future* tense by adding a thematic vowel, -b-, and a series of endings to the verb stem: **am-a-b-o** *I will love*, **am-a-b-is** *you will love* (**amare** *to love*). This way of marking the future does not survive in the modern languages.

In Standard Italian and Western Romance languages, the future tense is built upon the infinitive. Vulgar Latin speakers placed forms of the verb ***abere*** *to have* after the infinitive, which eventually turned into verb endings. Vulgar Latin ***fabulare a(be)s** (literally *to speak you have*) becomes Old Spanish **fablarás** *you will speak,* ***abere abio** *I have to have* turns into Italian **avrò** *I will have,* and ***parabolare abetis** *you all have to speak* produces Occitan **parlaretz** *all of you will speak.* The derivation is still clearly seen in Portuguese when the infinitive and ***abere** are split by an <u>object pronoun</u>: ***fabulare te abemus** (literally *to speak to you we have*) becomes **falar-te-emos** *we will speak to you.*

Future tense endings are limited to Western Romance. Romanian, Romansh, Sardinian, and Southern Italian do not share this feature. Romanian speakers may introduce a present <u>subjunctive</u> verb with **o să** to express the future: **o să mergi** *you will go.* Sardinian builds <u>helping verb</u> constructions out of Latin ***abere ad** *to have to* or ***debere** *ought* alongside an infinitive: Sardinian **des faeddare** or **as a faeddare** for *you will speak.* Romansh often uses the construction **vegnir ad** *to come to* with an infinitive for future actions: **el vegn ad esser** *he will be.*

Romance speakers also have ways of referring to the <u>near future</u>. These include <u>present tense</u> endings as well as constructions with <u>helping verbs</u> like *to go*: Italian **parliamo domani** *we'll speak tomorrow* (literally *we speak tomorrow*), **vado a parlare** *I'm going to speak* (literally *I go to speak*).

The verb tables at the end of this book list verbs in the future tense across many Romance languages.

Non-finite forms

All Romance languages have *<u>non-finite</u>* verb forms that do not indicate <u>person</u> and <u>number</u>. Three common forms are the infinitive (like English *to do*), the past participle (like *done*) and the gerund (like *doing*).

All Romance languages have *<u>infinitives</u>*. As discussed previously, languages inherit the <u>stem</u>-plus-<u>thematic vowel</u> system of Latin. This system gives modern languages three or four verb classes differentiated by a recurring vowel **a**, **e** or **i** after the verb stem. The infinitive ending **-r(e)** is added to the stem and thematic vowel: ***fabul-a-re**, Old Spanish **fablar**, Portuguese **falar** for *to speak*, but ***pot-e-re**, Italian **potere**, Spanish **poder** for *to be able.*

Some Romance languages have inflected infinitives or _personal infinitives_, which actually do carry information about the person and number of the subject: Portuguese **para falarmos**, Sardinian **pro faeddaremus** _for us to speak_. Such infinitives in languages like Galician, Portuguese, Sardinian, Old Leonese and Old Neapolitan have often been a topic of scholarly research.

The _past participle_ forms a completed adjective out of the verb. The Vulgar Latin masculine forms are ***-atu**, ***-etu**, ***-utu** and ***-itu** depending on the verb's thematic vowel: ***amatu**, Galician **amado**, Italian **amato** for _loved_ (***amare** _to love_), but ***servitu**, Italian **servito**, Galician **servido** for _served_ (***servire** _to serve_). Many languages have worn away the characteristic **-t-** within the past participle, at least in the masculine: Romansh **amà**, French **aimé**, Andalusian & Caribbean Spanish **amao** _loved_ (masculine) versus Romansh **amada**, French **aimée**, Andalusian & Caribbean Spanish **amá** _loved_ (feminine).

These past participles can act as adjectives to describe nouns, but they also play a key role in perfect and passive constructions in all languages: Romanian **avem vorbit** _we spoke / have spoken_, French **il a chanté** _he sang / has sung_, Spanish **fue escrito** _it was written_.

The _present participle_ ***-nte** forms an ongoing adjective from a verb. All languages have words derived from this Latin participle, but only some use it productively to create new adjectives: Italian **un'idea interessante** (**interessare**) _an interesting idea_ (_to interest_), **vocabolario parlante** (**parlare**) _speaking/conversational vocabulary_ (_to speak_).

The Vulgar Latin _gerund_ is built with the thematic vowel plus an ending ***-ndu**: ***fablandu**, Portuguese **falando** for _speaking_, or ***credendu**, Italian **credendo** for _believing_. This verb form may introduce an ongoing or surrounding action: Italian **parlando latino, il gruppo domanda...** _speaking Latin, the group asks..._ The present participle has fallen into disuse in some languages (like Spanish, Portuguese and Romanian), while in others the gerund and present participle have become identical (as in French and Catalan). The Italian and Iberian gerund is used with a helping verb in a progressive construction much like English _she is doing_: Italian **Maria sta parlando latino** _Mary is [in the process of] speaking Latin_, but French does not have ***Marie est parlant latin**.

The Romance verb tables at the end of this book include typical examples of non-finite verbs in many Romance languages.

Mood

Latin verb endings include information about the speaker's perspective or judgment of an action (_mood_). Verbs in the modern Romance languages still use endings to distinguish between a range of moods. The examples below assume acquaintance with <u>person-number</u> endings and verb <u>tenses</u>.

Indicative mood

The Latin and Romance _indicative_ is the basic mood and has a range of uses. The most widely used mood, the indicative allows the speaker to present a verb in a matter-of-fact way: Latin ***scitis**, Sardinian **ischides**, Romanian **ştiţi** for _all of you know_. Indeed, the indicative often marks a straightforward statement or question: Vulgar Latin ***parabolas latinu?**, Italian **parli latino?**, French **tu parles latin ?** use the indicative to ask _do you speak Latin?_, while ***parabolo latinu**, Italian **parlo latino**, French **je parle latin** also use the indicative to respond _I speak Latin_.

The versatility of the indicative is matched by the number of tenses that appear in this mood. Verbs have <u>present</u>, <u>past</u>, <u>imperfect</u> and <u>future</u> endings in the indicative. The other Romance moods are limited to one or two tenses, and are usually associated with a single tense.

The examples below compare a handful of usage situations where the indicative mood predominates.

Latin	Spanish	Romanian	
*Cantat bene.	Canta bien.	Cântă bine.	_He sings well._
*Cantat bene!	Canta bien!	Cântă bine!	_He sings well!_
*Cantat bene?	¿Canta bien?	Cântă bine?	_Does he sing well?_
*Cantat bene.	Canta bien.	Cântă bine.	_He sings well._

Latin	Spanish	Romanian	
*Non cantat bene.	No canta bien.	Nu cântă bine.	*He doesn't sing well.*

The Romance verb tables at the end of this book include multiple examples of tenses in the indicative. The comparison of present indicative forms is a good place to start.

Subjunctive mood

Latin and Romance verbs let a speaker mark an action that is wanted, hoped, doubted, feared, recommended or in any way not necessarily the case. In this mood, the speaker is no longer making factual statements or questions as in the indicative, but implying that something is possibly contrary to the facts. Verbs have this quality when put in the *subjunctive* mood. To form the subjunctive, verbs normally switch their thematic vowel (a becomes e/i and e/i turns into a): Latin *cantet, Spanish cante, Italian canti *(that) he sing* versus Latin *cantat, Spanish canta, Italian canta *he sings*, and Latin *veniat, Spanish venga, Italian venga *(that) he come* versus Latin *venit, Spanish viene, Italian viene *he comes*.

The Romance languages routinely place **que/che** to the left of the subjunctive. The word acts somewhat like *that* in *I know that he's happy*. When the statement before **que** indicates that what comes next may be contrary to fact, the subjunctive is expected to follow in all languages: Vulgar Latin ***parabolat latinu** *she speaks Latin* but ***volio quod parabolet latinu** *I want her to speak Latin* (literally *[I] want that [she] speak Latin*). The subjunctive is normally buried behind a secondary *that*-phrase after an indicative verb. In this use, a subjunctive verb is not the first verb in the sentence. The subjunctive is "triggered" by the meaning of an earlier verb.

Statements introducing a fact, like *know that, say that, remember tha,* or *hear that,* are commonly followed by an indicative verb. Statements expressing emotions or uncertainty, such as *prefer that, hope that, doubt that* or *need that,* normally precede a subjunctive verb. The following sample sentences contrast a *that*-phrase followed by an indicative with a *that*-phrase triggering a subjunctive.

	indicative mood	subjunctive mood
Vulgar Latin	***vidio quod cantas**	***spero quod cantes**
Portuguese	**vejo que cantas**	**espero que cantes**
Sardinian	**vido chi cantas**	**ispero chi cantes**
	I see that you sing	*I hope that you sing*

Romanian extends the use of the subjunctive to any verb that follows the word **să**. Like the surrounding non-Romance languages of the Balkans, Romanian links two finite verbs where other Romance languages have an <u>infinitive</u>: **pot să merg** *I can go* (literally *I can that I go*), **putem să vorbim** *we can speak* (literally, *we can that we speak*). While Romanians can say **putem vorbi** (literally *we can to speak*), by contrast, no Western Romance speaker has access to structures like Catalan ***podem que parlem** *we can that we speak.*

The subjunctive also provides a milder substitute for the <u>imperative</u> mood: Spanish **que vengas** *(that you) come* rather than the more direct **¡ven!** *come!* or French **que tu parles** *(that you) speak* instead of the stronger **parle!** *speak!* Like other uses of the Romance subjunctive, this hedged command may be translated with the English verb *may* or *could*: Spanish **que tú vengas acá por favor** *could you come here, please.* Notice that the **que** is retained before the subjunctive in most but not all cases: **vive la France !** *long live France!* (literally *[may] France live*).

The subjunctive verbs in this discussion have all appeared in the present tense. Many Romance speakers also use an <u>imperfect</u> tense in the subjunctive mood, which similarly marks an ongoing action in the past as counterfactual: Catalan **esperava que parlessin** *he was hoping that they spoke* versus **espera que parlin** *he hopes that they speak.* The imperfect subjunctive frequently appears in unreal *if*-phrases like *if I were*: Vulgar Latin ***si ego parabolasse**, Italian **se io parlassi**, literary French **si je parlasse** for *if I spoke.*

Old Spanish, Portuguese and Galician have a <u>future</u> subjunctive as well. These endings are used when the verb contains information about the future that is uncertain or contrary to fact: Portuguese **se voltarmos do Brasil...** *if we return from Brazil...* or **quando fores grande**

when you are big / will be big. Future subjunctive endings resemble the
<u>inflected infinitive</u>, but verb forms are actually close to the third-
person plural of the <u>past tense</u>: Old Spanish **facer** *to do*, past tense
ficieron *they did*, future subjunctive **que ficieres** *that you [will] do*.

The Romance verb tables at the end of this book demonstrate the
present subjunctive and imperfect subjunctive of verbs in many
Romance languages.

*Old church in Bârsana, Romania. The Romanian verb **ruga**
appears in the indicative mood in **se roagă** ("he prays") and the
subjunctive in **vrea să se roage** ("he wants to pray").*

Imperative mood

The Latin *imperative* issues a direct command: ***parabola** speak!* All
Romance languages inherit imperative forms: Romansh **dà!**, Spanish
¡da!, Sardinian **da!**, Romanian **dă!** *give!* or Romansh **dai!**, Spanish
¡dad!, Sardinian **dade!**, Romanian **dați!** *(all of you) give!*

French, Franco-Provençal, Rhaeto-Romance and Romanian can use the <u>plural</u> commands to address a single person politely or formally: French **parlez!** *speak!*, Romanian **veniți!** *come!*

Languages that can issue <u>polite</u> third-person commands use the present subjunctive for that purpose: Italian **parlino!**, Catalan **parlin!** *all of you speak! (formal)*. Iberian languages also use the subjunctive for negative commands: Portuguese **não fales!** *do not speak (informal)*, **não fale!** *do not speak (formal)*.

The grammar tables at the end of this book include a comparison of verbs in the imperative mood throughout the Romance languages.

Conditional mood

The <u>conditional</u> marks a hypothetical, like English *I would go*. Latin does not have unique endings dedicated to the conditional, but Western Romance languages with a set of <u>future</u> endings also mark the conditional: Western Vulgar Latin ***(tu) parabolare abes** *you have to speak* becomes French **tu parleras**, Catalan **(tu) parlaràs** *you will speak*, while Western Vulgar Latin ***(tu) parabolare abebas** *you had to speak* becomes French **tu parlerais**, Catalan **(tu) parlaries** *you would speak*.

Just like the future tense, the Western Romance conditional adds a series of endings to the <u>infinitive</u> instead of the verb's <u>stem</u>. The Italian conditional endings derive from the <u>simple past</u> ***abui** *I had*, but the <u>imperfect</u> ***abeba** *I used to have* is used in French, Spanish and other Western Romance languages.

	future indicative	conditional
Western Romance	***saper-a(be)s**	***saper-abe(b)as**
Galician	**saberás**	**saberías**
Occitan	**saupràs**	**saupriás**
French	**tu sauras**	**tu saurais**
Italian Romance	***saper-abes**	***saper-abuisti**
Italian	**saprai**	**sapresti**

	future indicative	conditional
Dalmatian	**te sapare**	
	you will know	*you would know*

The introduction and fulfillment of a hypothetical phrase (the protasis and the apodosis) require the imperfect subjunctive alongside the conditional: ***si parabolasses latinu quid dicere abebas?**, Catalan **si parlessis llatí què diries?**, Italian **se parlassi latino che diresti?** *if you spoke Latin what would you say?*

In Eastern Romance languages, which normally lack a conditional, imperfect verb forms are used in both halves of the statement: some Northern Italian **se parlassi latino cosa dicevi**, Romanian **dacă vorbeai latineşte ce ziceai?** both translate literally as *if you were speaking Latin what were you saying?* Other dialects allow the conditional in both halves: some Southern Italian **se parleresti latino cosa diresti?**, nonstandard French **si tu parlerais latin quoi tu dirais?** both literally mean *if you would speak Latin, what would you say?* Romanian commonly uses a construction with Latin ***abere** *have*: **dacă ai vorbi latineşte ce ai zice**, literally *if you have to speak Latin what [do] you have to say?*

The Romance verb tables at the end of this book compare conditional endings among languages that have them.

AUXILIARIES "HAVE" & "BE"

The two Vulgar Latin verbs for *have* and *be* are sometimes found on their own as a main verb. They are also brought in as secondary support for another main verb. In cases of support, they act as helping verbs, occurring directly beside and giving information about a main verb, like the English *has* in *she has spoken* or *was* in *it was written*. As with all Romance verbs, ***abere** and ***essere** carry information about person-number, tense-aspect and mood. Since *have* and *be* carry the finite information expected from a verb, a main verb supported by ***abere/*essere** is used in a simple non-finite form.

*abere for "have"

The regular Latin verb ***abere** *to have* also occurs in the modern languages: Romansh **vus avais diesch amis**, French **vous avez dix amis**, Italian **voi avete dieci amici** translate to *all of you have ten friends*. While often used with the basic meaning *possess*, Romance ***abere** also helps form new constructions out of other verbs. The most basic of these constructions resemble English *have done* or *has written*.

The table on the next page compares Romance forms of ***abere** in the <u>present indicative</u>. French verb forms are listed with pronouns since French verbs, like English (and other Romance languages, including Romansh and Emiliano-Romagnolo), require <u>subject pronouns</u>. The longer Romanian forms are used with possession but not for the <u>perfect</u>: **(voi) aveți o limbă** *all of you have a language* but **(voi) ați vorbit** *all of you have spoken*.

The Ibero-Romance languages retain ***abere** for the perfect but not as the general verb meaning *to possess*: Spanish **han aprendido** *they have learned* but not ***han dinero** *they have money*. For the meaning *possess*, Iberian languages prefer ***tenere** *to hold*: Portuguese **têm dinheiro**, Galician **teñen diñeiro**, Extremaduran **tienin dineru** for *they have money*. Indeed, Portuguese speakers even opt for Latin ***tenere** instead of ***abere** as a helping verb: **ela tem falado** is preferred to the older **ela há falado** for *she has spoken*.

The Western Romance languages use third-person <u>singular</u> forms of ***abere** (and singular forms only) to point out the <u>existence</u> of something or someone (English *there is / there are*): Portuguese **havia duas mulleres**, Galician **había duas mulleres** *there were two women* (literally *[it] had two women*), while plural forms like **haviam duas mulheres** only appear in nonstandard speech. Most of these languages use a small location word ***ic** *there* alongside ***abere** to indicate existence: French **il y a quatre langues**, Catalan **hi ha quatre llengües**, Old Spanish **ha y quatro lenguas** *there are four languages* (precisely *[it] there has four languages*).

Latin	Romanian	Italian	Corsican	Sardinian	French	Occitan	Catalan	Spanish	Portuguese	
*abere	avea	avere	avè	àere	avoir	aver	haver	haber	haver	*to have*
*abio	am	ho	aghju	apo	j'ai	ai	he	he	hei	*I have*
*a(be)s	ai	hai	ai	as	tu as	as	has	has	hás	*you have*
*a(be)t	a(re)	ha	hà	at	il/elle a	a	ha	ha	há	*he/she has*
*abemus	a(ve)m	abbiamo	avemu	amus	nous avons	avèm	hem	hemos	havemos	*we have*
*abetis	a(ve)ți	avete	avete	adzis	vous avez	avètz	heu	habéis	haveis	*all of you have*
*a(be)nt	au	hanno	ani	ant	ils/elles ont	an	han	han	hão	*they have*

*essere for "be"

The Latin verb *essere is a highly irregular verb found in all of the modern languages. Like the English verb *be*, Vulgar Latin *essere can link two items in a sentence: *illa idea est bona, Leonese la idea ye bona, Romanian idea e(ste) bună *the idea is good*. Also, like *be* in English *be done* or *is written*, the Romance *essere is used with other verbs to form constructions with a main verb: Vulgar Latin *est scriptu, Catalan és escrit, Italian è scritto *[it] is written*.

The table on the next page compares the <u>present indicative</u> forms of *essere across the Romance languages. As already mentioned, *essere functions as a *copula* or linking verb in the Romance languages. This is the expected function when *essere is found as a main verb: Catalan això és un club, Romanian acesta este un club *this is a club*. When followed by certain <u>nouns</u>, including those that reference affiliations or professions, <u>indefinite articles</u> are typically omitted: French elle est médecin *she is [a] doctor*, Spanish eras amigo de Juan *you were [a] friend of John*.

Iberian languages have multiple verbs that cover the sense of *be*. These languages distinguish between characteristic or long-term *being* with *essere from temporary *being* with *stare: Spanish es seguro *it is safe* (essential characteristic) versus está seguro *it is/seems safe* (current state). The Iberian use of *stare is especially common for location: Latin *stant in Roma, Catalan estan en Roma, Portuguese estão em Roma *they are in Rome*.

This strong distinction between *essere and *stare—both meaning *be*—holds from Catalonia to Portugal. Corsican stà, Sardinian istare and Italian stare share some of these properties.

Central and Eastern Romance languages use *essere to point out the <u>existence</u> of someone or something (English *there is / there are*): Italian c'è una lingua *there is a language* and ci sono quattro lingue *there are four languages*, or Romanian e(ste) o limbă *[there] is a language* and sunt patru limbi *[there] are four languages*. Western Romance languages instead employ *abere for this purpose.

Latin	Romanian	Italian	Corsican	Sardinian	French	Occitan	Catalan	Spanish	Portuguese	
*essere	fi	essere	esse	èssere	être	èsser	(és)ser	ser	ser	*to be*
*su(m)	sunt	sono	sò	soe	je suis	soi	sóc	soy	sou	*I am*
*es	eşti	sei	sè	ses	tu es	ès	es	eres	és	*you are*
*est	e(ste)	è	hè	est	il/elle est	es	és	es	é	*he/she is*
*sumus	suntem	siamo	semu	semus	nous sommes	sèm	som	somos	somos	*we are*
*estis	sunteţi	siete	seti	sedzis	vous êtes	sètz	sou	sois	sois	*all of you are*
*sunt	sunt	sono	sò	sun	ils/elles sont	son	són	son	são	*they are*

Perfect verb forms

Modern Romance languages use ***abere** or both ***abere** and ***essere** with a past participle to mark that an action has been completed. Like English *has spoken*, the action of the main verb in these *perfect* constructions was completed at one point in time. A speaker uses the perfect to look back to that completed action from a later point in time.

All languages have a construction equivalent to *has done*. Languages build this construction with the past participle of the main verb: Vulgar Latin ***parabolatu**, Italian **parlato**, Catalan **parlat**, French **parlé** *spoken*. The past participle follows the verb ***abere**: ***abere parabolatu**, Italian **avere parlato**, Catalan **haver parlat**, French **avoir parlé** *to have spoken*. The verb ***abere** then picks up the grammatical information normally expected from the main verb: Latin ***abet parabolatu**, Catalan **ha parlat**, French **il a parlé**, Italian **ha parlato** *he has spoken* versus Latin ***abent parabolatu**, Catalan **han parlat**, French **ils ont parlé**, Italian **hanno parlato** *they have spoken*.

The periphery languages of the East (Romanian) and the West (Iberian) form the perfect with ***abere** as described above. Sardinian, Corsican, French, Swiss and Italian Romance use ***abere** as the basic helping verb for the perfect, but rely on ***essere** in marked contexts. Those marked contexts predominantly include verbs that take no direct object, such as verbs indicating movement (*come, go, fall,* and so on): ***su arrivatu**, Corsican **sò arrivatu**, Sardinian **so arrivau**, Italian **sono arrivato**, French **je suis arrivé** *I have arrived* (literally *I am arrived*), or ***est arrivatu**, Corsican **hè arrivatu**, Sardinian **est arrivau**, Italian **è arrivato**, French **il est arrivé** *he has arrived* (literally *he is arrived*).

When languages form a perfect with ***essere** and a past participle, the past participle acts like an adjective describing the subject. Like other Romance adjectives, the past participle's ending matches the number and gender of the verb's subject. The next examples compare perfects with ***essere** plus a past participle. Counterexamples from non-***essere** languages (Spanish and Romanian) provide contrast.

	masculine	feminine	masculine plural	feminine plural
Latin	***est venitu**	***est venita**	***sunt venitos/veniti**	***sunt venitas/venite**
Romansh	**el è vegnì**	**ella è vegnida**	**els èn vegnids**	**ellas èn vegnidas**

	masculine	feminine	masculine plural	feminine plural
Italian	è venuto	è venuta	sono venuti	sono venute
French	il est venu	elle est venue	ils sont venus	elles sont venues
Sardinian	est venidu	est venida	sun venidos	sun venidas
	he is come	*she is come*	*they are come*	*they (all fem.) are come*
Latin	*abet venitu	*abet venitu	*abent venitu	*abent venitu
Spanish	ha venido	ha venido	han venido	han venido
Romanian	a venit	a venit	au venit	au venit
	he has come	*she has come*	*they have come*	*they (all fem.) have come*

Again, the *essere-language participles match the <u>gender</u> and <u>number</u> of the subject. Plural forms ending in -i/-e (as in Italian) come from the Latin <u>nominative</u>, while plurals in -s (as in Sardinian) come from the Latin <u>accusative</u>. Languages that have <u>plural nouns</u> ending in -s have plural past participles ending in -s. Likewise, languages that have plural nouns with a vowel ending also have plural past participles with the same ending. Also, the past participle in some of the above languages is *venutu instead of *venitu.

Languages using *essere and *abere presumably recognize the past participle as an adjective more than languages only having *abere. Its role as an adjective is further supported when *essere-languages use *abere with a <u>direct object pronoun</u>, as in English *has cooked it*. In these situations, the past participle agrees with the object: *illa abio criticata, Sardinian l'apo criticada, French je l'ai critiquée *I have criticized her* or *illos abio criticatos, Sardinian los apo criticados, French je les ai critiqués *I have criticized them*. Languages that only use *abere for the perfect largely lack this kind of agreement: *illa abio criticatu, Spanish la he criticado *I have criticized her* but not *la he criticada.

In Sardinian, Romanian (but not Aromanian), Swiss, French and Italian Romance, the perfect has become the default <u>past tense</u>: Vulgar Latin *abes vistu, Sardinian as vistu, French tu as vu, Italian hai visto, Romanian ai văzut for *you saw*. The Iberian languages still draw a distinction between perfects and preterits: Portuguese perfect tenho amado *I have loved* versus simple past amei *I loved*. Outside Iberian and Aromanian, the inherited simple past is confined to literary or (in Italy) regional use: French **il parla**, Italian **lui parlò** *he spoke* occur in formal literature, while French **il a parlé**, Italian **ha parlato** *he spoke* are common in conversation.

Catalan speakers regularly use modified forms of the verb *go* with an <u>infinitive</u> to form the past: Catalan **vaig cantar en llatí** *I sang in Latin* and **vares parlar** *you spoke*. Catalan still maintains both a simple past and a separate perfect construction: Catalan perfect **he cantat** *I have sung* versus literary past **cantí** *I sang* (written/formal).

The discussion so far fails to assign the perfect to any specific <u>tense</u> or <u>mood</u>. This is because all languages are able to form perfects with all tenses and moods of ***abere/*essere**, which results in tremendous flexibility but also a proliferation of perfect "tenses": Galician **hei cantado** *I have sung*, **había cantado** *I had sung / used to have sung*, **haberei cantado** *I will have sung* and so on. The use of these composed and supercomposed tenses is especially common in languages like French that wholly rely on perfect forms for expressing the past tense (as in the examples following ***abes vistu** above).

The next table compares forms of the perfect in various tenses and moods. The example verb ***venire** *come* is chosen because it gets its support from ***essere** in Sardinia, Corsica, France, Italy and Switzerland but ***abere** in Spain, Portugal and Romania.

tense-mood	Spanish	Occitan	Italian	
present indicative	**ha venido**	**es vengut**	**è venuto**	*he has come*
present subjunctive	**...que haya venido**	**...que siá vengut**	**...che sia venuto**	*...that he have come*
imperfect indicative	**había venido**	**èra vengut**	**era venuto**	*he had come*
future indicative	**habrá venido**	**serà vengut**	**sarà venuto**	*he will have come*
conditional	**habría venido**	**seriá vengut**	**sarebbe venuto**	*he would have come*

The difference between simple past and imperfect is one of <u>aspect</u> (*had* once versus *had* ongoing). The aspect is less clear in the past perfect (English *had done*), where speakers generally prefer the imperfect plus a past participle. The Romance past perfect more often goes by the name *pluperfect,* or Latin **plus quam perfectum** *more than completed.* Some languages have pluperfect verb endings instead of the helping verb construction seen above: Portuguese **cantara**, Romanian **cântase** *he had sung.* The endings are literary in Portuguese, and speakers stick to forms like **tinha cantado** *he had sung* in conversation. Speakers of Standard Romanian (Daco-Romanian) use pluperfect verb endings, while Aromanian has the helping verb construction.

"To have to"

Some Romance languages also couple ***abere** with an infinitive. The resulting construction reads like English *have to (do).* Unlike English *to have to,* the Romance construction does not express obligation in all languages that contain it.

Unlike Western Romance, Sardinian lacks a set of future tense endings. Sardinian speakers make use of Latin ***abere ad** *to have to* plus an infinitive to talk about the future: **as a cantare** *you will sing* or **apo a faeddare** *I will speak.* Sardinian may also employ the verb ***debere** *ought* with an infinitive to mark the future: **des cantare** *you will sing.*

More often, ***abere** and an infinitive form expressions of relevance or obligation: French **ils ont à faire**, Catalan **han de fer**, Galician **hai que facer** *they have to do.* The Romanian equivalent uses a past participle instead: **am de făcut** *I have to do* (literally *I have of done*).

The Latin verb ***debere** is also common for expressing obligation: French **il doit chanter**, Portuguese **deve cantar**, Italian **deve cantare** *he should/must sing.* Also popular are impersonal verb phrases with *lack* or *need*: French **il faut** *it is necessary*, **il me faut** *I must*, **il me faut chanter** *I must sing* or Romanian **trebuie** *it is necessary*, **îmi trebuie** *I must*, **îmi trebuie să cânt** *I must sing* (using the Romanian subjunctive).

Romanian uses modified forms of ***abere** before an infinitive to mark the conditional. These conditional forms have become distinct from the expected forms of the verb **avea** *have*: **aş cânta** *I would sing* but not ***am cânta** (versus the perfect **am cântat** *I sang / have sung*).

Perfect of reflexive verbs

When the subject and object of a verb are identical, Romance languages use a <u>reflexive pronoun</u> for the object, like English *themselves* in *saw themselves*.

Some Romance languages (like French and Italian) form the <u>perfect</u> forms of a verb using either the supporting verb *abere *have* or *essere *be*. Other languages (like Spanish and Portuguese) only use *abere in the perfect. Languages that use *essere tend to expect *essere instead of *abere in perfect forms of reflexive verbs: Italian **si è lavata**, French **elle s'est lavée**, Romansh **ella è sa lavada** *she washed herself* instead of French *elle s'a lavé.

Iberian and Romanian languages do not form the perfect with *essere and do not expect agreement between the subject and the past participle of a reflexive verb: Romanian **ea s-a spălat** *she washed herself*, Spanish **ella se ha lavado** *she has washed herself*.

Passive voice with past participle

The Latin and Romance <u>past participle</u> can be used in a *passive* sense, much as in English: Latin *scriptu, Italian **scritto**, Romanian **scris**, Portuguese **escrito**, Romansh **scrit** *written*. A full passive phrase involves the verb *essere *be* and the past participle: Vulgar Latin *est scriptu, Italian **è scritto**, Romanian **e scris**, Portuguese **é escrito** *[it] is written*. The passive agent may be brought out with the local equivalent of *by*: Italian **fu scritto da Anna**, Portuguese **foi escrito por Ana** *[it] was written by Anna*.

Romansh prefers to form the passive with the Latin verb *venire *come* instead. Like *essere, the Romansh verb **vegnir** is followed by a past participle in passives: **i vegn scrit** *it is written* (literally *it comes written*).

The Romance languages are generally inclined to express the passive in other ways. Universally, the most popular technique appropriates the reflexive to form the passive: Vulgar Latin *se cantat ad sic, Spanish **se canta así** *it is sung this way* (literally *[it] sings itself this way*), or Vulgar Latin *illa lingua se parabolat in Europa, Italian

la lingua si parla in Europa for *the language is spoken in Europe* (literally *the language speaks itself in Europe*).

Historic Kotor, Montenegro, once home to the extinct Dalmatian language.
*The past participle of the Dalmatian verb **frabicur** (Latin **fabricare**)*
*appears in the passive phrase **joi frabicuat** ("[it] is built").*

The Romance verb tables at the end of this book include a comparison of past participles across representative languages.

Common phrases with *abere and *essere

The Romance languages form a number of common phrases with the verb ***abere**. These phrases describe the state of a person and involve a noun with a <u>zero article</u> where English instead has an adjective: Italian **ho fame** *I am hungry* (literally *I have hunger*), **ho ragione** *I am right* (literally *I have reason*). The Iberian languages use ***tenere** instead, which has become the normal Iberian verb for *have*: Spanish Portuguese **tenho fome** *I am hungry* (*I have hunger*), **tenho razão** *I am right* (*I have reason*).

The lack of an article is a key feature of such expressions: Italian **ho bisogno di sapere** (literally *I have need of to know*), Romanian **am nevoie să ştiu** (*I have need that I know*) for *I need to know*. This is true of these expressions even in languages that rarely use <u>zero articles</u> (like

French): French **j'ai besoin de savoir** *I need to know* also translates precisely to *I have need of to-know*.

Romanian uses the verb ***essere** *be* with an object pronoun to form many (but not all) of these expressions: **mi-e foame** *I am hungry* (literally *to-me is hunger*) but **am dreptate** *I am right* (*I have correctness*).

The table below compares the expressions *I am hungry*, *I am cold* and *I am right* across the Romance languages.

Portuguese	**tenho fome**	**tenho frio**	**tenho razão**
Spanish	**tengo hambre**	**tengo frío**	**tengo razón**
Catalan	**tinc fam**	**tinc fred**	**tinc raó**
French	**j'ai faim**	**j'ai froid**	**j'ai raison**
Romansh	**jau hai fom**	**jau hai fraid**	**jau hai raschun**
Italian	**ho fame**	**ho freddo**	**ho ragione**
Sardinian	**appo famine**	**appo fridu**	**appo rejone**
Romanian	**mi-e foame**	**mi-e frig**	**am dreptate**
	I am hungry	*I am cold*	*I am right*

HELPING VERBS

The Romance languages build many verb constructions that bring in a secondary verb to support a main verb. These secondary helping verbs fall directly beside and give information about a main verb, like the English *can* in *she can speak* or *need* in *you need to write*. In such situations, the helping verbs carry information about <u>person-number</u>, <u>tense-aspect</u> and <u>mood</u>. Since they carry the finite information expected from a verb, a main verb supported by a *helping verb* occurs in a simple <u>non-finite</u> form, just like *to speak* or *to write*.

Two major Romance helping verbs are ***essere** *be* and ***abere** *have*. Their key role in Romance grammar has earned these two verbs their own dedicated section in this book. Flip through the previous pages for more information about them.

Progressive aspect with *stare

As discussed in the introduction to *essere *be*, some Romance languages use two *be* verbs: *essere for existence or essence versus *stare for a temporary state or location. Languages with the verb *stare tend to use it along with the <u>gerund</u> to build an expression paralleling English *to be doing*. The Latin verb *stare shows some irregularities in the modern languages. The table below lists the <u>present indicative</u> forms of the verb.

Latin	Portuguese	Spanish	Catalan	Italian	
*stare	estar	estar	estar	stare	*to be (state/location)*
*sto	estou	estoy	estic	sto	*I am*
*stas	estás	estás	estàs	stai	*you are*
*stat	está	está	està	sta	*he/she is*
*stamus	estamos	estamos	estem	stiamo	*we are*
*statis	estais	estáis	esteu	state	*all of you are*
*stant	estão	están	estan	stanno	*they are*

In the <u>progressive</u> construction, *stare is used as a helping verb, while the main verb appears as a gerund: Vulgar Latin *cantandu, Italian cantando, Portuguese cantando *singing* and then Vulgar Latin *sto cantandu, Italian sto cantando, Portuguese estou cantando *I am singing*.

Sardinian has the same progressive construction, but uses *essere instead of *stare with the present gerund. Sardinian speakers make frequent use of this progressive: ses vidende *you are seeing*. Indeed, speakers include the progressive even where English speakers prefer the simple verb: a lu ses vidende *do you see it?*

Occitan and European Portuguese build the progressive with the verb *be* followed by *ad plus an <u>infinitive</u>. Occitan uses *essere, while Portuguese relies on *stare for this progressive: Occitan èsser a cantar, Portuguese estar a cantar *to be singing*, or Occitan es a cantar, Portuguese está a cantar *she/he is singing*.

Some Italian languages have different, unique ways of capturing the progressive aspect: Venetian semo drio far *we are doing* (literally *we are behind to do*), **drio tirar zxó** *downloading* (literally *behind to pull down*).

Speakers of all languages have access to the simple present tense for all types of present actions. Languages like French, Romansh and Romanian that lack ***stare** progressives can supply the present instead: Italian **parlo** *I speak* and **sto parlando** *I am speaking* versus French **je parle** *I speak / am speaking* (although a French speaker could take pains to clarify **je suis en train de parler** *I am in [the] process of speak[ing]*). This next table compares the progressive in a selection of tenses and moods.

tense-mood	Portuguese	Catalan	Italian	
present	está cantando	està cantant	sta cantando	*he is singing*
present subjunctive	...que esteja cantando	...que estigui cantant	...che stia cantando	*...that he be singing*
imperfect	estava cantando	estava cantant	stava cantando	*he was singing*
future	estará cantando	estarà cantant	starà cantando	*he will be singing*
conditional	estaria cantando	estaria cantant	starebbe cantando	*he would be singing*

As the examples above demonstrate, the progressive is not a verb tense but a separate feature of the verb that marks an action in progress. The Romance verb ***stare** can be placed in all combinations of tenses and moods, including even perfect forms. All of these juxtapositions give a progressive nuance to the resulting construction. The table below neatly compares a Romance verb with and without this progressive aspect marker.

	simple	progressive
Latin	***cantandu**	***stat cantandu**
Catalan	**canta**	**està cantant**
Romansh	**chanta**	
Italian	**canta**	**sta cantando**
French	**chante**	
	sings	*is singing*

Near future: "going to do"

Most modern languages have a way of talking about near events in the future, stating that an action *is going to* happen. This construction includes the Latin verb for *go* with an <u>infinitive</u>.

The Romance languages source their verb *go* from multiple Latin verbs. In most languages, some or all present-tense forms are inherited from ***vadere** *go / walk*. Infinitives, participles and some other verb forms employ ***ire** *to go* or the curious intermediary ***andare**, which might be rooted in Vulgar Latin ***ambitare** or ***amblare**. Iberian, Rhaeto-Romansh and Southern Italian languages combine ***ire** and ***vadere**. Catalan, Occitan, Italian and other languages combine ***andare** and ***vadere**. French also acts this way, but with ***alare** instead of ***andare**, and ***ire** in the <u>future</u> and <u>conditional</u>. Iberian languages also retain ***andare** as a separate verb.

Romanian uses many Latin verbs for personal movement, among them Latin ***mergere** *to immerse*: **mergi** *you go*, **mergem** *we go*. Sardinian simply has regular forms of ***andare**: **ando** *I go*, **andamus** *we go*, **andande** *going*, **andare** *to go*.

The next table compares representative forms of the verb *go* across several Romance languages.

Portuguese	Catalan	French	Italian	Sardinian	Romanian	
ir	anar	aller	andare	andare	merge	*to go*
vou	vaig	je vais	vado	ando	merg	*I go*
vais	vas	tu vas	vai	andas	mergi	*you go*
vai	va	il/elle va	va	andat	merge	*he/she goes*
vamos	anem	nous allons	andiamo	andamus	mergem	*we go*
ides	aneu	vous allez	andate	andates	mergeți	*all of you go*
vão	van	ils/elles vont	vanno	andant	merg	*they go*
ia	anava	il allait	andava	andaiat	mergea	*he used to go*
foi	vaig anar	je suis allé	sono andato	so andatu	am mers	*I went*
tenho ido	he anat	je suis allé	sono andato	so andatu	am mers	*I have gone*
estou indo	estic anant	je vais	sto andando	so andande	merg	*I am going*

Some Iberian languages place *ad before the infinitive to form the _near future_: Spanish **vamos a ver** _we are going to see_ versus Portuguese **vamos ver** _we are going to see_. Most of Romance uses _go_ directly before the infinitive: French **je vais chanter**, Italian **io vado cantare** _I am going to sing_.

Like Spanish, Catalan has the Iberian construction: Catalan **vaig a parlar anglès** _I am going to speak English_. However, speakers often prefer either the present or the future: **demà parlaré anglès** or **demà parlo anglès** for _tomorrow I [will] speak English_.

Romansh uses the same order but with **vegnir a(d)** _come to_ to talk about the future more generally (near or distant): **ti vegns ad esser** _you will be / are going to be_, **jau vegn ad ir** _I will go / am going to go_. Romanian speakers use a similar construction with modified forms of *volere _want_ and an infinitive for the general future: **voi cânta** _I will sing_, **tu vei cânta** _you will sing_, **veţi cânta** _all of you will sing_.

The near future contrasts with the basic future tense of Western Romance: Italian **vai andare** _you are going to go_ versus **andrai** _you will go_. Both of these futures differ from the <u>present tense</u>, which can introduce events relevant to the present but planned for the future: French **ça commence demain**, Sardinian **cumenzat cras**, Spanish **comienza mañana** _it starts tomorrow_.

Recent perfect: "just done"

The Romance languages also make use of helping verbs when expressing an action that was recently completed, like English _he just arrived_. Such constructions express a near or recent <u>perfect</u>.

Iberian languages build the near perfect with **acabar de** _to finish from_: Portuguese **acaba de chegar**, Catalan **acaba d'arribar** _he just arrived_. On the other hand, Gallic languages rely on **venir de** _to come from_: Occitan **ven d'arribar**, French **il vient d'arriver** _he just arrived_ (literally _he comes from arriv[ing]_).

Languages can also capture this meaning with an adverb _barely_ and the past tense: Spanish **apenas llegó** _he just arrived_, Italian **è appena arrivato** _he just arrived_ (literally _[he] is barely arrived_), or

Romanian **tocmai a plecat** *he just arrived* (literally *[he] barely has arrived*).

Modal verbs

Latinic languages mark some grammatical <u>moods</u> on the verb, but Romance speakers make their mood towards an action explicit by using a *<u>modal verb</u>* like *can, hope, wish, need* and so on: ***potet andare** > Sardinian **podet andare** *[she] can go*. Like all helping verbs, the modal verb is marked with the <u>person-number</u>, <u>tense-aspect</u> and grammatical <u>mood</u>. The main verb is left in the <u>infinitive</u>: Vulgar Latin ***tu voles cantare**, Occitan **tu vòls cantar**, Romansh **ti vuls chantar** *you want to sing*.

The following table contrasts the main verb ***parabolare** *speak* with and without a modal in various languages.

	main finite verb	main infinitive	modal + main verb
Vulgar Latin	***parabolo**	***parabolare**	***volio parabolare**
Catalan	**parlo**	**parlar**	**vull parlar**
Italian	**parlo**	**parlare**	**voglio parlar**
French	**je parle**	**parler**	**je veux parler**
	I speak	*to speak*	*I can speak*

The next examples display a variety of modal verbs across the Romance languages.

modal	Vulgar Latin	Spanish	Italian	Romanian	Sardinian	
can	***potet cantare**	**puede cantar**	**può cantare**	**poate cânta**	**podet cantare**	*he can sing*
want	***volet/querit cantare**	**quiere cantar**	**vuole cantare**	**vrea să cânte**	**cheret cantare**	*he wants to sing*
know how	***sapit/scit cantare**	**sabe cantar**	**sa cantare**	**ştie cânta**	**ischit cantare**	*he knows how to sing*

Romanian prefers modal constructions like **pot să cânt** (literally *I can that I sing*) and **vreau să cânt** (literally *I want that I sing*) instead of the infinitive. The second Romanian verb (here **cânta** *sing*) appears in the subjunctive.

The English equivalents sometimes require an intervening particle *to* between the modal verb and main verb: *I can go* versus *I want to go*. In the Romance examples above, the infinitive consistently falls just to the right of the main verb without any mandatory intervening elements. Actually, Romance does have phrasal verbs that require a preposition before the infinitive.

Perception verbs work like these modals in Romance, but the infinitive refers to a second subject (referenced by a direct object pronoun, just like Latin accusative+infinitive): Spanish **la veo cantar** *I see her sing*, Italian **ti ho visto partire** *[I] have seen / saw you leave*. As noted in the treatment of the subjunctive mood, Romance languages normally expect to separate two verbs with two different subjects into two finite phrases linked by *quod: Latin *scio quod venis, Galician **sei que venes**, Sardinian **isco chi venis** for *I know that you come / are coming*. Verbs of perception provide the principal exception to this expectation, but even these verbs have a counterpart with *quod: Vulgar Latin ***vidio quod cantas** or ***te vidio cantare**, Spanish **veo que cantas** versus **te veo cantar** for *I see that you sing / are singing* versus *I see you sing*.

Verbs with prepositions

Many Romance helping verbs can be followed by an infinitive. Some of these helping verbs, including verbs of modality and perception, take an infinitive directly. Other verbs expect some intervening element between the auxiliary and the infinitive. The intervening material is typically a preposition before the infinitive, most often Latin *ad *to* or *de *of*: French **je refuse de partir** *I refuse to leave* (but not just ***je refuse partir**), Italian **continuo ad imparare** *I continue to learn* (and not ***continuo imparare**). In comparison, English adds a similar element in *wants to speak* not found in *can speak*.

The choice of preposition depends on the first verb, not on the infinitive that follows: Italian **imparo a parlare** *I learn to speak*, **imparo a leggere** *I learn to read*, but not ***imparo di parlare**). To help distinguish *prepositional verbs*, dictionaries and learning materials often cite such verbs with their preposition: **imparare a** *to learn to*. This next table compares variations of the Romance prepositional helping verb ***comin(i)tiare ad** *begin to*.

	helping verb + preposition + infinitive
Vulgar Latin	***comintio ad cantare**
Spanish	**comienzo a cantar**
Portuguese	**começo a cantar**
Corsican	**cumenciu à cantà**
Sardinian	**cuminzo a cantare**
Italian	**comincio a cantare**
French	**je commence à chanter**
	I start to sing

Romanian provides a clear exception to this structure, having instead **incep să cânt** *I start that I sing*. This Romanian construction, which relies on the subjunctive, displays a characteristic Romanian pattern that contrasts with Central and Western Romance, including Italian and Dalmatian.

Pronouns

subjects, objects, possessives, impersonal

Classical Latin			
ego	*I*	nos	*we*
me	*me*	nos	*us*
mihi	*to me*	nobis	*to us*
mei	*mine*	nostri	*ours*

Romance personal pronouns still distinguish <u>subjects</u> from <u>objects</u>.

Pronouns have <u>possessive</u> forms, commonly used with nouns.

Personal pronouns have <u>person</u> and <u>number</u>. These singular and plural pronouns refer to the first person.

Vulgar Latin	
*nos vides	
you see us	
*inter nos	
between us	

Direct object and indirect object clitics are placed around the verb.

Strong object pronouns often follow prepositions.

Vulgar Latin	
*qui venit?	*who comes?*
*istu venit	*this comes*
*necunu venit	*no one comes*

Romance languages use demonstrative, interrogative and other <u>impersonal</u> pronouns.

FEATURES

Latin has short words that can be used in place of a more specific noun. These *pronouns* carry person, number and case information, and some also mark formality. The Romance languages inherit and build on the Latin pronoun system.

- The basic pronominal features are visible in Romance subject pronouns. Personal pronouns have numbers (like nouns), persons (like verbs), and sometimes gender (like nouns) and formality.

- Romance languages also have personal possessive and impersonal demonstrative, interrogative, relative and indefinite pronouns. These pronouns bear close relation to possessive, interrogative and demonstrative adjectives.

- Cases allow Romance languages to distinguish subject pronouns from object pronouns—strong object pronouns are more often used with a preposition, while weak object pronouns are used with a verb.

SUBJECT PRONOUNS

Latin *subject pronouns* distinguish between three persons—the speaker (first person), the person spoken to (second person) and a third person outside the conversation. They also distinguish two numbers—one individual (singular) versus multiple individuals (plural). The third-person pronouns also mark gender—masculine, feminine and neuter. The modern Romance languages expand and modify this system, variously introducing concepts like politeness or extending gender to other persons.

Traditionally, the gender and politeness features of Romance pronouns are treated together with person and number, a convention followed in this text.

Person, gender & politeness

Romance subject pronouns universally distinguish between three _persons_, starting with the speaker—the first person (_I_), the second person (_you_) and the third person (_he/she_). The first-person pronoun unambiguously derives from Latin ***ego**: Portuguese **eu**, Spanish **yo**, Occitan **ieu**, French **je**, Romansh **jau**, Sardinian **jeo** all mean _I_.

Most Romance languages subdivide the second person into _polite_ versus familiar pronouns. The Latin pronoun **tu** _you_ is used to address someone informally: Galician **ti**, Spanish **tú**, Italian **tu**, Sardinian **tue**, Romanian **tu** _you_. Iberian, Sardinian and Italian languages use third-person pronouns in polite contexts, such as a younger speaker addressing an older one: Italian **tu parli bene** _you (familiar) speak well_ versus **Lei parla bene** _you (polite) speak well_.

French and Swiss Romance use second-person plural verb forms to address a single person politely: French **vous chantez**, Romansh **Vus chantais**, Romanian **dumneavoastră cântați** _you (polite) sing_. Romanian also has a second-person singular form **dumneata** (shortened to **mata**) somewhere between the informal second-person singular and the polite use of the second-person plural **dumneavoastră**: Romanian **dumneata cânți** _you (polite) sing_ versus **dumneavoastră cântați** _you (very polite) sing_.

The polite Iberian pronouns derive from ***vostra mercede** _your grace_: Galician **vostede**, Portuguese **você**, Spanish **usted**, Catalan **vostè**, Sardinian **vosté**. Iberian, Sardinian and Italian polite pronouns relate to third-person verb forms: Italian **Lei canta** and not ***Lei canti**, Portuguese **você canta** but not ***você cantas**, Spanish **usted canta** and not ***usted cantas** for _you (polite) sing_. European Portuguese distinguishes between three levels of politeness: familiar **tu**, neutral **você** and a formal pronoun. The formal pronoun is **o senhor** _sir_ when addressing a male and **a senhora** _madam_ to address a female. As in other languages, the non-**tu** pronouns relate to third-person verb forms: Portuguese **o senhor canta** but not ***o senhor cantas** for _you (formal) sing_.

Spanish speakers in much of Latin America have a second-person pronoun **vos**. For some speakers, **vos** replaces **tú**: Rioplatense **vos cantás** for Standard Spanish **tú cantas** _you sing_. For other speakers, the two pronouns distinguish different types of relationships: Guatemalan **vos cantás** (between males) versus **tú cantas** (intimate or between females). **Vos** and **tú** both contrast with the polite **usted**.

Don Quijote and Sancho Panza in Madrid. Don Quijote addresses Sancho as **tú**, but Sancho responds with **vuestra merced** ("your grace").

The social conditions that dictate the speaker's choice of second-person pronoun are complex and vary from language to language. Generally, when the relationship between addresser and addressee is close, speakers use the pronoun **tu** and second-person verb forms. When the addressee or both the speaker and addressee are younger, the occurrence of **tu** becomes more frequent. Speakers are even conscious of a clear line between familiar and polite address: French **tutoyer**, Portuguese **tratar por tu**, Spanish **tutear** and Italian **dare del tu** mean *to address [someone] as "tu"*.

The third-person pronouns distinguish between masculine and feminine gender, just like English *he* and *she*. These normally derive from the <u>nominative case</u> of Latin **ille** *that man* and **illa** *that woman*: Portuguese **ele** *he* versus **ela** *she*, French **il** *he* versus **elle** *she*, or Romanian **el** *he* versus **ea** *she*. (<u>The accusative case</u> of these same Latin words turns into the <u>definite article</u> in most of Romance.) The Standard Italian counterparts derive from late <u>dative case</u> forms **illei* *to that woman* and **illui* *to that man*: **lui** *he* versus **lei** *she*. Sardinian takes its third-person pronouns from **isse* and **issa* (Classical **ipse** and **ipsa**) instead: Sardinian **isse** *he* versus **issa** *she*.

The third-person pronouns are substituted for inanimate nouns of the same gender: French **la voiture, elle marche** *the car, it works* (literally *the car, she works*). The masculine also serves as the <u>default gender</u>: French **il marche** *it works* (where *it* does not refer to a specific gendered noun). Their ability to render English *it* suggests that Romance third-person pronouns are simply masculine and feminine pronouns, not strictly animate pronouns corresponding to *he* and *she*.

<u>Neuter</u> third-person pronouns also exist in a number of languages. These are used for a generic *it* or *that* and treated as grammatically masculine: Spanish **ello**, French **ça**, Catalan **això**, Occitan **açò**, Italian **ciò**, Romansh **i** for *it*. Rhaeto-Romance can use the invariable **i** (**igl** before a vowel) as a generic third-person pronoun: **ella chanta bain** *she sings well* versus **i chanta bain** *he/she/it sings well*.

Many languages have a third-person pronoun that references a general subject, similar to the indefinite use of English *one* in *one learns a language*. French speakers use such a pronoun to form the <u>passive</u> and as the conversational first-person plural *we*: **on apprend** *we learn / it is learned*. Likewise, Romansh **ins** plays an indefinite role in a sentence: **ins chanta bain** *one sings well*. Other languages tolerate similar structures: Spanish **uno aprende** *one learns*, literary Catalan **hom parla** *one speaks*.

Along with its normal third-person pronouns **ea** *she* and **el** *he*, Romanian has the polite pronouns **dumnealui** *he* and **dumneaei** *she*.

Some Romance languages can echo or *<u>reinforce</u>* subject pronouns: Venetian **ti te parla vèneto** *you (emphatic) speak Venetian*, French **toi, tu parles français** *you (emphatic) speak French* (literally *you you speak...*). Also, some languages regularly reinforce a subject <u>noun</u> with a third-person pronoun: Rhaeto-Romansh **mes bab l'è là** *my father he is there*.

In a few languages, including French and Romagnolo, subject pronouns typically lean against and are pronounced together with their verb: French **je parle** or even colloquial **j'parle** for *I speak*.

The Romance pronoun tables at the end of this book compare subject pronouns across various languages.

Number, gender & politeness

Pronouns in Latin and the Romance languages distinguish between one individual (like *I*) and multiple individuals (like *we*). The first-person singular pronouns from Latin **ego** have a corresponding plural from Latin **nos**: Portuguese **nós**, Italian **noi**, French **nous**, Sardinian **nois** *we*. Some Western Romance languages compound *nos with *altros *others* to form the pronoun, especially in Central and Eastern Iberia: Spanish **nosotros**, Catalan **nosaltres** *we*. The feminine form *nos altras refers to an all-female group: Spanish **nosotras**, Catalan **nosaltres** *we (all female)*. French speakears prefer the third-person singular **on** in conversation: colloquial **on parle** for standard **nous parlons** *we speak*.

The second-person plural corresponding to singular **tu** is the Latin **vos**: French **vous**, Sardinian **vois**, Galician **vós**, Italian **voi** for *all of you*. Languages that form first-person plurals with *nos altros have a corresponding second-person plural *vos altros *you others*: Spanish **vosotros** *all of you*, **vosotras** *all of you (all female)*.

The Romance languages take fewer pains to distinguish politeness in the plural. Italian continues to use a third-person pronoun for polite address: **voi parlate** *all of you speak* versus **Loro parlano** *all of you (polite) speak*. In Iberia and Sardinia, speakers generally draw a distinction between the familiar *vos (altros) and polite *vostra mercedes: Catalan **vosaltres** *all of you (familiar)* versus **vostès** *all of you (polite)*. European Portuguese, which once separated familiar **vós** from neutral **vocês** and polite **os senhores**, has lost **vós** over the past century. Similarly, most Latin American speakers use the once-formal **ustedes** as the plural form of address in all situations.

Languages that use the second-person plural to politely address a singular person do not always extend formality to the plural: French **vous chantez** corresponds to Italian **voi cantate** *all of you (familiar) sing* and **Loro cantano** *all of you (formal) sing*. Romanian speakers use the polite pronoun **dumneavoastră** for both singular and plural address: **voi cântați** *all of you speak* versus **dvs. cântați** *all of you (polite) speak*.

The next two tables compare formal, neutral and polite second-person pronouns across representative languages.

	European Portuguese		European Spanish		Latin American Spanish	
	singular	plural	singular	plural	singular	plural
familiar	**tu**	**vocês**	**tú**	**vosotros**	**tú / vos**	**ustedes**
neutral	**você**					
formal	**o senhor /** **a senhora**	**os senhores /** **as senhoras**	**usted**	**ustedes**	**usted**	

	Brazilian Portuguese		French		Italian		Romanian	
	singular	plural	singular	plural	singular	plural	singular	plural
familiar	**você**	**vocês**	**tu**	**vous**	**tu**	**voi**	**tu**	**voi**
neutral			**vous**		**Lei**	**Loro**	**tu / dumneata**	
formal	**o senhor**	**a senhora**					**dumneavoastră**	

The third-person plural pronouns come from plural forms of Latin **ille** *that man* and **illa** *that woman*. As with plural nouns, Eastern Romance languages use the nominative forms *ille *those women* and *illi *those men*, while Western languages employ the accusatives *illas and *illos: Spanish **ellos** *they* versus **ellas** *they (all feminine)*, but Romanian **ei** *they* versus **ele** *they (all feminine)*.

The masculine pronouns also act as the *default gender*. French **ils**, Spanish **ellos**, Romanian **ei** and Catalan **ells** all mean *they* for a group of males, a mixed group of males and females and even a group of unknown gender. Feminine plural pronouns like Catalan **elles** and Romanian **ele** are used for a group composed entirely of females or feminine nouns.

Italian again derives its plurals from the late genitive *illoru *of them*, which does not vary for gender: **loro** *they* (masculine and feminine). Sardinian relies on *issos and *issas for its third-person plurals: **issos** *they* versus **issas** *they (all females)*.

In addition to **ei** and **ele**, Romanian also has the polite third-person pronoun **dumnealor**.

The pronoun tables at the end of this book compare singular and plural subject pronouns across the Romance languages.

OBJECT PRONOUNS

Romance pronouns have distinct object forms corresponding to Latin accusative and dative cases. Like subject pronouns, these *object pronouns* carry information about person, number and, in some cases, gender and politeness. The modern languages use small object pronouns alongside a verb when the pronouns act as a direct (accusative) or indirect (dative) object of that verb. Languages employ a different set of emphatic or strong object pronouns when the pronoun is the object of a preposition like *for me*.

Direct object pronouns

The Romance verb takes object pronouns that sit near and are pronounced together with it. When the Romance verb takes a *direct object*, a direct object pronoun is normally placed to the left of the verb: Romansh **el ma vesa**, Italian **(lui) mi vede**, Romanian **(el) mă vede** *he sees me*. Direct object pronouns contain information about person and number just like subject pronouns: Spanish **me ve** *he sees me* (singular) versus **nos ve** *sees us* (plural), **me ve** *sees me* (first person) versus **te ve** *sees you* (second person). Third-person object pronouns derive from Vulgar Latin **illu* and **illa*, the accusative forms of **ille* *he* and **illa* *she*. These distinguish between masculine and feminine gender: Italian **lo vedo** *I see him* versus **la vedo** *I see her*, and **li vedo** *I see them* versus **le vedo** *I see them (all females)*.

Languages that use third-person subjects to address a second person politely do the same with third-person objects: Spanish **usted ve** *you (formal) see* corresponds to **lo ve** *I see you (formal)*, which, depending on context, also means *I see him*. Likewise, languages that use second-person plural subjects to address someone politely use second-person plural objects for the same purpose. For instance, the subject of French **vous voyez** *you (formal) see* corresponds to the object of **je vous vois** *I see you (formal)*.

Crucially, generic third-person subjects do not always relate to a third-person object pronoun. For example, the French subject **on** *one/we* corresponds to the first-person object **nous** in **il nous voit** and not the third-person **le** in **il le voit* for *he sees us*.

The Romance grammar tables at the end of this book contain a comparison of direct object pronouns across the Romance languages. Also, the section on the syntax of <u>verb phrases</u> explores the placement of object pronouns around the verb.

Indirect object pronouns

The Romance languages treat objects directly impacted by the verb differently than objects removed from the verb's action, like the direct object *him* in *I saw him* versus the indirect *to him* in *I gave it to him*. Like direct objects, *<u>indirect object pronouns</u>* sit near and are pronounced together with the verb: Italian **la vedo** *I see her* (direct) versus **gli dico** *I say to her* (indirect).

The first-person and second-person indirect object pronouns are identical to their direct object forms: Spanish **me ve** *sees me* and **me dice** *says to me*, Italian **ti vede** *sees you* and **ti dice** *says to you*. Third-person direct objects come from **illi*, the <u>dative</u> of both **ille* *he* and **illa* *she*: Vulgar Latin **illi dico*, Italian **gli dico**, Spanish **le digo** *I say [to] him/her*. Corresponding plurals exist: Vulgar Latin **illis dico*, Romanian **le zic**, Spanish **les digo** *I say [to] them*. French uses the dative form **illui* *to him / to her* instead: French **je lui dis** *I say to him/her*. French also inherits the <u>genitive</u> plural **illoru* *of them* as an indirect object meaning *to them*: French **je leur dis** *I say to them*.

The choice between direct and indirect objects is based on the verb's meaning, and does not necessarily match English: Spanish **lo espero** *I wait for him* (direct in Romance, indirect in English) versus **le ruego** *I ask him* (indirect in Romance, direct in English). The third-person direct object pronouns do not mark masculine or feminine gender: Spanish **le doy el libro** *I give the book to her*, where **le** can represent *to him*, *to her* or *to it*, or plural **les doy el libro** *I give the book to them*, where **les** represents *they* in any gender.

Uniquely, the Romanian languages continue to distinguish between direct (<u>accusative case</u>) and indirect (<u>dative</u>) objects in nearly all persons and numbers: Romanian **mă vede** *he sees me* but **îmi zice** *he says to me.*

Daily menu for an Italian restaurant. Italians inherit *illu as a direct object pronoun in lo servono ("[they] serve it"). Compare the phrase gli servono ("[they] serve you"), which uses *illi as a polite indirect object pronoun.

As with <u>direct object pronouns</u>, whenever a language contains <u>polite</u> forms of address for subject pronouns, corresponding object pronouns exist: the subject of Spanish **usted dice** *you (formal) say* corresponds to the indirect object of **le digo** *I say to you (formal),* and the subject of French **vous parlez** *you (formal) speak* corresponds to the object of **je vous parle** *I speak to you (polite).*

The Romance grammar tables at the end of this book contain a comparison of indirect object pronouns in representative Romance languages. Also, the section on the syntax of <u>verb phrases</u> explores the placement of object pronouns around the verb.

Reflexive object pronouns

The set of reflexive pronouns looks and works like direct or indirect <u>object pronouns</u> in Romance, but with a critical difference: reflexives have the same person and number as the <u>subject</u> of the verb. In other words, speakers use *reflexive objects* when the subject and the object of a verb are identical: Romansh **jau ma lav** *I wash myself*, French **il se lave** *he washes himself*, Romanian **ne spălam** *we wash ourselves*. Like indirect object pronouns, the only surface difference between reflexives and other object pronouns exists in the third-person forms. The third-person reflexive pronoun comes from Latin *se in all languages.

The reflexive pronouns can represent either <u>direct</u> or <u>indirect</u> reflexive objects in most of Romance without any difference in form: Spanish **él se da cuenta** *he realizes* (*he gives to-himself account*, with an indirect object) versus **él se lava** *he washes himself* (direct object). Uniquely, Romanian reflexive pronouns distinguish direct objects from indirect objects: **el își dă seama** *he remembers* (literally *he gives to-himself account*, with an indirect object pronoun) versus **el se spală** *he washes himself* (direct object).

The bond between reflexive pronouns and verbs expressing a reflexive action is tight in Romance. Romance reflexive verbs always take a reflexive pronoun: French **je me rase** but not just ***je rase** for *I shave (myself)*, as French **je rase** expects some object. Romance languages express reflexivity whenever possible, and many verbs that are reflexive in Romance have no corresponding reflexive form in English: Italian **ti senti bene** *you feel well* (literally *[you] feel yourself well*). The next table compares verbs with reflexive and non-reflexive objects in selected languages.

	Spanish	Romansh	Sardinian	Romanian	
direct obj.	**lo lava**	**el al lava**	**lu samunat**	**îl spală**	*he washes it*
reflexive direct obj.	**se lava**	**el sa lava**	**si samunat**	**se spală**	*he washes himself*

	Spanish	Romansh	Sardinian	Romanian	
indirect obj.	**lo da**	**el al dat**	**lu dat**	**îl dă**	*he gives it*
reflexive indirect obj.	**se da**	**el sa dat**	**si dat**	**îşi dă**	*he gives himself*

Languages with a generic third-person pronoun use the third-person reflexive pronoun ***se** rather than first-person ***nos**: French **on se lave** has the reflexive meaning *we wash ourselves*, while **on nous lave** means *one washes us / we are being washed*.

The Romance grammar tables at the end of this book compare reflexive object pronouns across the languages. Also, the introduction to sentence structure explores the placement of object pronouns within <u>verb phrases</u>, which equally applies to reflexive objects.

Strong object pronouns

Languages also have stressed object pronouns that do not revolve around the verb, like English *me* in *for me*. These <u>*strong object pronouns*</u> are most often found after <u>prepositions</u>: Spanish **para mí** *for me* instead of the standard "weak" object pronoun ***para me**. A few languages allow strong objects in isolation or to repeat the subject for emphasis: French **moi?** *me?* or **moi, je chante** *I (emphatic) am singing* versus Spanish **¿yo?** but not ***¿mí?** for *me?* and **canto yo** but not ***mí yo canto** for *I (emphatic) am singing*.

The majority of these strong object pronouns coincide with <u>subject pronouns</u>: Spanish **ella canta**, Italian **lei canta** *she sings* and Spanish **para ella**, Italian **per lei** *for her*. However, the first and second-person singular strong object pronouns are usually different: Italian **io canto**, Romanian **eu cânt** *I sing* versus Italian **per me**, Romanian **pentru mine** *for me*.

As mentioned, strong objects are usually found after non-verb words, particularly prepositions. Swiss Romance languages allow strong objects to follow a verb as well: Romansh **jau ves tai** (strong object pronoun) and **jau ta ves** (with a <u>weak object pronoun</u>) both mean *I see you*, and **per tai** means *for you*.

<u>Prepositional phrases</u> can reinforce or emphasize the indirect object: Spanish **a él le gusta** *he (emphatic) likes it* (literally *to him to-him*

pleases). Languages with a <u>personal accusative</u> construction also use prepositional phrases to mark a direct object: Ladin **veder ad el** *to see him*, or Spanish **la vemos a ella**, Romanian **o vedem pe ea** *we see HER* (literally *her we-see to her*).

The Romance grammar tables at the end of this book include a comparison of these strong prepositional object pronouns across various languages.

POSSESSIVE PRONOUNS

Possessive pronouns agree with the <u>number</u> and <u>gender</u> of a noun, working primarily as <u>possessive adjectives</u>. The main difference is that possessive pronouns occur without a noun and often with an article, while possessive adjectives sit alongside a noun: Portuguese **o meu** *mine* versus **o meu nome** *my name*, Romanian **numele meu** *my name* (neuter) versus **al meu** *mine* (masculine/neuter). In a few languages, the possessive pronouns have a different shape than the possessive adjectives: Spanish **mi opinión** *my opinion* (feminine) versus **la mía** *mine* (feminine), or French **mon avis** *my opinion* (masculine) versus **le mien** *mine* (masculine), although conversational French has **à moi** *to me* for *mine*.

The Romanian countryside. Like other Romance speakers, Romanians use possessives to speak of **patria mea** *("my fatherland").*

The table below compares the singular possessives *my*, *your* and *his* in Romance. In all languages but Romanian, the third-person possessive stands for *his*, *hers* and *its*, but Romanian uses the genitive pronouns **lui** *of him* and **ei** *of her* instead of Latin ***suu** *his/her*.

		Sardinian		Spanish		French		Italian		Romanian	
		sing.	pl.	sing.	pl.	sing.	pl.	sing.	pl.	sing.	pl.
1st sing.	masc.	**meu**	**meos**	**mi**	**mis**	**mon**	**mes**	**mio**	**miei**	**meu**	**mei**
	fem.	**mea**	**meas**			**ma**		**mia**	**mie**	**mea**	**mele**
2nd sing.	masc.	**tuo**	**tuos**	**tu**	**tus**	**ton**	**tes**	**tuo**	**tuoi**	**tău**	**tăi**
	fem.	**tua**	**tuas**			**ta**		**tua**	**tue**	**ta**	**tale**
3rd sing.	masc.	**suo**	**suos**	**su**	**sus**	**son**	**ses**	**suo**	**suoi**	**lui**	
	fem.	**sua**	**suas**			**sa**		**sua**	**sue**	**ei**	

This next table presents plural possessives in multiple languages.

		Sardinian		Portuguese		French		Romanian	
		sing.	pl.	sing.	pl.	sing.	pl.	sing.	pl.
1 pl.	m.	**nostru**	**nostros**	**nosso**	**nossos**	**notre**	**nos**	**nostru**	**noştri**
	f.	**nostra**	**nostras**	**nossa**	**nossas**			**noastră**	**noastre**
2 pl.	m.	**vostru**	**vostros**	**vosso**	**vossos**	**votre**	**vos**	**vostru**	**voştri**
	f.	**vostra**	**vostras**	**vossa**	**vossas**			**voastră**	**voastre**
3 pl.	m.	**issoro**		**seu**	**seus**	**leur**	**leurs**	**lor**	
	f.			**sua**	**suas**				

The first-person plural possessive relies on Latin ***nostru** *our*, the second on ***vostru** *[all of] your*, and the third person either on ***suu** *their* (in Spanish, Portuguese and Corsican) or ***illoru** *of them* (in most of Romance, including French, Romansh, Italian and Romanian). Portuguese and Latin American Spanish have largely replaced the second-person plural with polite third-person forms: Portuguese **vocês têm suas ordens** versus the archaic **vós tendes vossas ordens** for *all of you have your orders*. Sardinian again chooses ***isse** instead of ***ille** for its third-person forms: Sardinian **issoro** *their*. Catalan and

Occitan have both ***suu** and ***illoru** in the third-person plural: Catalan **seu** *their* (standard) or **llur** *their* (literary).

As discussed above, each possessive has multiple forms corresponding to the <u>number</u> and <u>gender</u> of the possessed noun: Italian **suo** *her* matches the masculine noun **figlio** *son* in **suo figlio** *her son* but the feminine noun **figlia** *daughter* in **sua figlia** *her daughter*. Romanian <u>neuter nouns</u> match masculine forms in the singular but feminine ones in the plural: **cuvântul meu** *my word* versus **cuvintele mele** *my words* (where **cuvânt** *word* is neuter). <u>Noun phrases</u> with possessives require a <u>definite article</u> before the possessive in some languages (as in Catalan and Romanian), but the possessive replaces the article in other languages (like French and Spanish).

IMPERSONAL PRONOUNS

Demonstrative pronouns

The Romance languages use a set of <u>*demonstrative pronouns*</u> derived from Latin ***istu**, ***issu** and ***illu**. In general, demonstratives built with ***istu** refer to something near the speaker, and those with ***issu** or ***illu** to something distant from the speaker. These demonstratives function as deictic elements that point to a location: Portuguese **isto** versus **isso** Italian **questo** versus **quello** for *this* (near me) versus *that* (near you). Iberian languages have a third location for nouns distant from the speaker and the addressee: Portuguese **aquilo** *that over there* (distant from both of us).

French has collapsed the distances, so that the same pronoun refers to all locations: **celui** translates to both *this* and *that*. Speakers can clarify by marking the pronoun with **-ci** *here* or **-là** *there*: **celui-ci** *this here* or **ceci** *this*, and **celui-là** *that there* or **cela** *that*.

The demonstrative pronouns typically agree with the gender of a noun, so they act like <u>demonstrative adjectives</u>: Italian **questa canzone è bella** *this song is beautiful* alongside **questa è bella** *this [one] is beautiful* (where **questa** *this [one]* agrees with a <u>feminine noun</u>).

Interrogative & relative pronouns

Interrogative pronouns allow speakers to ask an explicit question about an unknown <u>subject</u> or <u>object</u>: Vulgar Latin ***quid voles?**, Catalan **què vols?**, Italian **che vuoi?** *what [do] you want?* Question pronouns can act as both subject and object of verb: colloquial French **t'as vu qui ?** *who[m] did you see?* (literally *you have seen who?*), **qui dort là ?** *who sleeps there?* Both subject and object interrogatives tend to open these kinds of <u>wh-questions</u>, just as in English: Spanish **¿qué quieres?**, Romanian **ce vrei?** *what [do] you want?* (with the interrogative object *what?* at the front) as opposed to the abnormal Spanish **¿quieres qué?** *you want what?* The form of Romance question words typically remains constant whether they act as object or subject, as seen with French **qui** *who/whom* in the previous examples.

Romance speakers also have access to <u>interrogative adjectives</u> like Vulgar Latin ***quantos** *how many?*, ***quales** *which?* and <u>adverbs</u> like ***quando?** *when?* Interrogative pronouns and adjectives are closely related to the *relative pronouns* that introduce <u>dependent clauses</u>, notably ***quod**: Latin ***sapio quod sapis quod...**, Portuguese **sei que sabes que...**, Italian **so che sai che...** *I know that you know that...* Other relatives have wide currency, too: French **l'homme qui dort** *the man who sleeps / is sleeping* Romanian **un film care l-am văzut** *a movie that I saw* (literally *a film which it [I] have seen*, with object pronoun <u>reinforcement</u>). Relatives contrast with interrogatives: Italian **quando sei a casa?**, Spanish **¿cuándo estás en casa?** *when are you at home?* versus **quando sei a casa**, **cuando estás en casa** *when you are at home*.

Indefinite pronouns

Romance languages use *indefinite pronouns* to make a non-specific reference. Many of these pronouns contain the word for *some*, like English *someone* or *something*: French **quelque chose**, Italian **qualcosa**, Portuguese **alguma coisa** *something* (literally *some thing*). Universal pronouns are built with ***totu** *all*: French **tout le monde**, Spanish **todo el mundo**, Portuguese **toda a gente**, Romanian **toată lumea** *everyone* (literally *all the world/people*).

<u>Negative</u> forms of these pronouns also exist. These negatives tend to contain the word *no* or *none*: Portuguese **nenhuma coisa** *nothing*,

Italian **nessuno** *no one*, Romanian **niciodată** *never*, Romansh **nagut** *nothing*. French languages draw some of their negative indefinites from terms that initially had a positive value: Latin ***re(s)*** *thing* versus Catalan **res** *nothing*, and ***persona*** *person* versus French **personne** *nobody*.

Indefinite <u>determiners</u> like ***paucu*** *little/few*, ***multu*** *much/many*, ***altru*** *other*, ***totu*** *all* may double as indefinite pronouns. Also, French **on**, Romansh **ins** and similar generic third-person pronouns are grouped with indefinites.

Adjectives & Adverbs

number, gender, comparatives, superlatives, adverbs

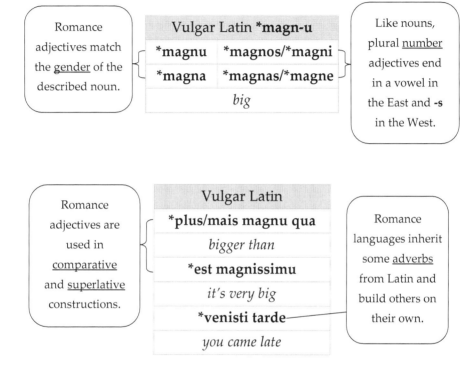

Romance adjectives match the <u>gender</u> of the described noun.	Vulgar Latin ***magn-u**		Like nouns, plural <u>number</u> adjectives end in a vowel in the East and **-s** in the West.
	*magnu	*magnos/*magni	
	*magna	*magnas/*magne	
	big		

Romance adjectives are used in <u>comparative</u> and <u>superlative</u> constructions.	Vulgar Latin	Romance languages inherit some <u>adverbs</u> from Latin and build others on their own.
	*plus/mais magnu qua	
	bigger than	
	*est magnissimu	
	it's very big	
	*venisti tarde	
	you came late	

FEATURES

- Latin uses *adjectives* to describe <u>nouns</u>. These adjectives match the <u>number</u>, <u>gender</u> and <u>case</u> of the described noun. The modern Romance languages inherit this way of forming and using adjectives, but have mainly lost the case distinctions and the <u>neuter</u> gender found among Latin adjectives.

- In addition, Romance languages build comparative and superlative phrases out of these basic adjectives.

- The Romance languages can turn adjectives into <u>adverbs</u>, just as English builds *fluently* from *fluent*.

ADJECTIVES

Agreement with Nouns

The basic Romance adjective has a <u>*stem*</u>, which relates its meaning, and an ending that matches the <u>number</u> and <u>gender</u> of the described noun. For example, the Itaian adjective **vera** in **idea vera** *true idea* has a stem **ver-** and a feminine singular ending **-a** that matches the feminine singular noun **idea**. The same adjective appears as masculine singular **vero** in the phrase **fatto vero** *true fact*. The same sort of <u>*agreement*</u> applies in singular and plural numbers: Italian **fatto vero** *true fact*, **fatti veri** *true facts*. The adjective continues to agree even when it is removed from the noun, like after ***essere** be*: Italian **il fatto è vero** *the fact is true* versus **i fatti sono veri** *the facts are true*.

Each language's treatment of number and gender endings on adjectives corresponds to that same language's treatement of noun number and gender. Languages that lose masculine endings and weaken feminine noun endings do the same with adjectives: Vulgar Latin ***bonu omu** becomes Romanian **bun om** *good person*, and ***bona casa** becomes Romanian **bună casă** *good house*. Likewise, languages that form noun plurals in ***-s** and those that form noun plurals with a vowel do the same with adjectives: Spanish **buena idea** *good idea* and **buenas ideas** *good ideas* versus Italian **buona idea** *good idea* and **buone idee** *good ideas*.

While the choice of gender and number ending depends on the noun described, the choice of adjective can restrict the variety of endings available. In particlar, languages have <u>*four-form adjectives*</u> that derive from Vulgar Latin adjectives with a masculine singular ending ***-u** and feminine singular ***-a**. On the other hand, Vulgar Latin adjectives with a singular ***-e** for all genders typically have <u>*two forms*</u> in the modern languages: Portuguese **um feito importante** *an important fact* and **uma ideia importante** *an important idea* versus **feitos**

importantes *important facts* and **ideias importantes** *important ideas.* The next table compares four-form adjectives versus two-form adjectives in Italian, which exemplifies the general Romance treatment of adjectives.

	four-form adjective		two-form adjective	
	masculine	feminine	masculine	feminine
singular	**buono**	**buona**	importante	importante
plural	**buoni**	**buone**	importanti	importanti
	good		*important*	

Again, Western Romance languages form plurals with the Late Latin <u>accusative</u> plural ***-s**: Spanish **ideas importantes** instead of Italian **idee importanti**. Most languages that have eroded the masculine and feminine endings, the masculine singular of adjectives in ***-u** and those in ***-e** now simply end in a consonant: Vulgar Latin ***bonu** becomes French **bon**, Romanian **bun** *good*, while ***importante** becomes French **important**, Romanian **important**. In such languages, many two-form adjectives have been adopted into the set of four-form adjectives: French **un fait important** *an important fact* (masculine) versus **une idée importante** *an important idea* (feminine), which presupposes an underlying difference between masculine ***importantu** versus feminine ***importanta**. Spanish, Italian and Portuguese have a single form **importante** for both genders.

Even Romanian, with its third <u>neuter gender</u>, still has four-form instead of six-form adjectives. Romanian neuters correspond to masculine adjectives in the singular and feminine adjectives in the plural. Similarly, Western Romance two-form adjectives still have two forms in Romanian, since they fail to distinguish gender. The following table demonstrates a Romanian four-form adjective **bun** *good* and a two-form adjective **mare** *big*.

	four-form adjective			two-form adjective		
	masculine	feminine	neuter	masculine	feminine	neuter
singular	**bun**	**bună**	**bun**	mare	mare	mare
plural	**buni**	**bune**	**bune**	mari	mari	mari

In all languages, the masculine form also acts as the _default gender_ when a gendered noun is lacking: French **il est important que** _it is important that_ has masculine **important**, not feminine ***elle est importante que**, just as Portuguese **é preciso que** _it is necessary that_ is not said ***é precisa que**.

This French sign warns trespassers with an adjective **interdit** ("forbidden") describing a masculine noun **chantier** ("site"). The feminine form of this adjective is **interdite**. Its plurals are **interdits** and **interdites**.

All languages can productively form adjectives from verbs. The past participle of a verb is a four-form adjective. For example, Vulgar Latin **amare** _to love_ gives the adjective ***amatu** _loved_: Italian **è amato** _he is loved_ versus **è amata** _she is loved_. Speakers use this past participle as an adjective to build one of the passive constructions.

Most adjectives follow the noun, such as **materna** in Spanish **una lengua materna** _a native language_. Some adjectives normally precede the noun instead, like **buena** in Spanish **una buena idea** _a good idea_. Romance languages have a specific way of structuring a noun phrase that determines the placement of the adjective relative to the noun and article.

Quantifiers and qualifiers also act like adjectives. These are typically found before the noun: Vulgar Latin ***illa metissima idea**, French **la même idée**, Portuguese **a mesma ideia**, Italian **la medesima idea** *the same idea* or Vulgar Latin ***una altra idea**, French **une autre idée**, Italian **un'altra idea**, Romanian **o altă idee** *another idea*. These include adjectives related to <u>indefinite pronouns</u> like ***totu** *all* and ***multu** *much*: Spanish **todas las casas**, Catalan **totes les cases**, Romansh **tuttas las chasas**, Italian **tutte le case** *all the houses* or Spanish **muchas casas**, Catalan **moltes cases**, Romansh **bleras chasas**, Italian **molte case** *many houses*.

Comparatives & superlatives

Latin adjectives take *comparative* endings to suggest that a description fits one noun better than another and *superlative* endings to characterize a description as best fitting a specific noun: Latin **citus**, **citior**, **citissimus** *fast*, *faster*, *fastest* (masculine forms). English continues to use related comparative endings, like the *-er* in *faster*, and superlative endings, like the *-est* in *fastest*. The Romance languages lose this set of adjective endings, and instead rely on phrases parallel to *more than* for the comparative and *the most* for the superlative.

The modern languages place either Latin ***plus** or ***mais** (both mean *more*) before an adjective for the comparative structure: Spanish **más importante**, Portuguese **mais importante**, Italian **più importante**, French **plus important** *more important*. Comparisons with *less* use either the Latin ***minus** or an expression *more small*: Spanish **menos importante**, French **moins important**, Italian **meno importante** *less important* versus Sardinian **prus pagu importante**, Romanian **mai puțin important** *less important* (literally *more small important*).

When placed before a compared noun, the comparative <u>particle</u> ***qua** *than* is appended to the adjective construction: French **c'est plus important que**, Romansh **igl è pli important che**, Spanish **es más importante que** for *it is more important than*. Italian languages and Sardinian use ***de** *of* for the comparative particle instead: Standard Italian **è più alto di**, Sardinian **est prus mannu de** *is taller than*. Romanian uses the comparative particle **decât**: **e mai important decât** *is more important than*.

Superlatives mimic the comparative construction, but add a <u>definite article</u>: Romansh **il pli impurtant**, Italian **il più importante**, Portuguese **o mais importante**, Spanish **el más importante** *the most important*. Romanian adds a definite article **cel** before the adjective and the noun, departing from its usual placement of the definite article after the noun: **românul** *the Romanian* but **cel mai bun român** *the best Romanian*.

Most of the Romance languages retain some irregular comparative forms: Vulgar Latin ***illu meliore**, Spanish **el mejor**, Italian **il migliore** *the best* rather than ***il plus/mais bonu**. However, Romanian does have **mai bun** *better* and **cel mai bun** *best*. Some languages also allow a productive superlative ending ***-issimu**, although this is normally reinterpreted as emphatic rather than superlative: Spanish **es buenísimo**, Italian **è buonissimo** mean *it's so good* rather than *it's the best*.

The Romance syntax tables at the end of this book include examples of comparative sentences throughout the language family.

ADVERBS

All languages have a fixed set of <u>adverbs</u> inherited from Latin words or phrases: Vulgar Latin ***bene** becomes Romanian **bine** and French **bien**, ***ac ora** *at this time* becomes Portuguese **agora** *now*, ***eri** becomes Italian **ieri** and Spanish **ayer** *yesterday*, and so on. This small set of words contains many adverbs of time, location and quality. Below are some Romance examples that share a common Latin root.

Latin	Spanish	Old French	Romansh	Italian	Sardinian	Romanian	
*odie	hoy	huy	oz	oggi	oje	azi	*today*
*bene	bien	bien	bain	bene	bene	bine	*well*
*ic	aquí	ici	qua	qui	innoghe	aici	*here*
*tarde/ *tardivu	tarde	tard	tard	tardi	tardu	târziu	*late*
*illac	allá	la	là	là	(igùe)	(acolo)	*there*

The Western Romance languages can also build adverbs productively. They do this by adding the ending **-mente** to the end of a feminine adjective: Spanish **claro** and **claramente**, Italian **chiaro** and **chiaramente** for *clear* and *clearly*. The adjective is turned into a true adverb, often used to modify a verb: Spanish **Juana habló claramente** *Jane spoke clearly*. By contrast, Romanian simply uses the <u>default</u> form of the adjective as an adverb: **învață inteligent** *she learns intelligently*.

In Romance languages, adverbs tend to appear after and close to the verb. Other elements and <u>phrases</u> may follow the adverb: French **Jeanne parle bien latin** but not *****Jeanne parle latin bien** for *Jane speaks Latin well*.

Particles

prepositions, conjunctions, interjections & others

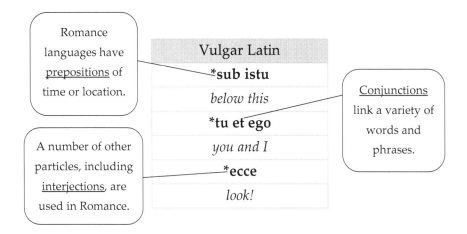

Romance languages have prepositions of time or location.

Vulgar Latin
*sub istu
below this
*tu et ego
you and I
*ecce
look!

Conjunctions link a variety of words and phrases.

A number of other particles, including interjections, are used in Romance.

FEATURES

Latin and the Romance languages contain a range of words that are not verbs, nouns, pronouns or adjectives. Most of these leftovers are small, invariable words that may be termed *particles*.

PREPOSITIONS

Romance *prepositions* are particles placed before a noun to mark time or location relative to that noun: Vulgar Latin *supre illu muru *above the wall*, *in illa casa *in the house*, *(ab)ante de ire *before going* (here with an infinitive). When the time or location is relative to a pronoun instead of a noun, Romance speakers use the prepositional form of the pronoun (the strong object pronoun): Spanish a mí, French à moi, Italian a me *to me*. The next table offers a examples of prepositions.

Latin	Portuguese	Catalan	French	Sardinian	Italian	Romanian	
*pro/*per	por	per	pour	pro	per	pe	*for*

Latin	Portuguese	Catalan	French	Sardinian	Italian	Romanian	
*ad	a	a	à	a(d)	a(d)		to
*de	de	de	de	de	di	de	of
*supre/*supra	sobre	sobre	sur	subra	sopra	spre	over
*cu(n)	com			cun	con	cu	with

CONJUNCTIONS

Latin and Romance have a basic set of _conjunctions_ that link two items, including but not limited to nouns and sentences: Vulgar Latin ***illu verbu et illa phrase** _the word and the sentence_, ***fablat bene mais non cantat bene** _she speaks well but she does not sing well_. Languages also use more sophisticated connectors to nuance a sentence or connect it to a larger body of speech: Spanish **sin embargo, no pude escapar** _nevertheless, I could not escape_, French **or il est désormais interdit** _still, it is henceforth prohibited_. The following table compares some of the common Romance conjunctions.

Latin	Portuguese	Spanish	French	Italian	Sardinian	
*et	e	y	et	e	e	_and_
*per oc		pero		però	parò	_but/however_
*mais	mas	mas	mais	ma	ma	_but_
*si	se	si	si	se	si	_if_
*aut	ou	o	ou	o	o	_or_

OTHER PARTICLES

Latin and the Romance languages employ miscellaneous particles, including _interjections_: Latin **ei** _yikes!_, French **aïe !** _ouch!_, Italian **to'** _here!_ (in the sense of _take it_), Romanian **măi** _hey!_ (for attention) and so on. The negative particle ***non/*ne** is used before a verb to negate it: Vulgar Latin ***non canto**, Romanian **nu cânt**, Portuguese **não canto** _I don't sing_. Other words are sometimes classed as particles, including articles and adverbs.

Sentences

noun phrases, verb phrases, basic sentences, compound sentences

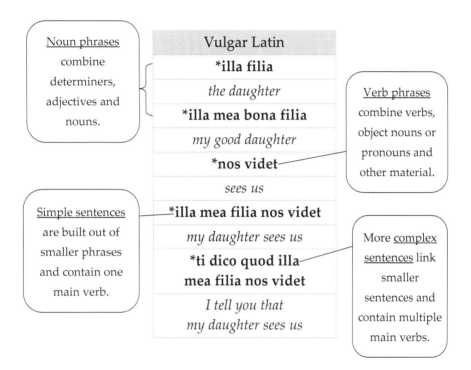

Noun phrases combine determiners, adjectives and nouns.

Vulgar Latin

illa filia
the daughter

illa mea bona filia
my good daughter

nos videt
sees us

illa mea filia nos videt
my daughter sees us

ti dico quod illa mea filia nos videt
I tell you that my daughter sees us

Verb phrases combine verbs, object nouns or pronouns and other material.

Simple sentences are built out of smaller phrases and contain one main verb.

More complex sentences link smaller sentences and contain multiple main verbs.

FEATURES

The following sections focus on the _syntax_—the word order and structure—of common types of phrases and sentences in Vulgar Latin and Romance.

- All languages build <u>noun phrases</u> with attention to the ordering of nouns, articles, adjectives and possessives.

- Languages build <u>verb phrases</u> with particular attention to the ordering of <u>pronouns</u> around the verb, including phrases with multiple object pronouns and reflexive pronouns.

- Basic sentences inclue affirmative statements, negative statements, questions and commands.

- Romance languages form compound sentences (including sentences with a second verb in the indicative, subjunctive or infinitive mood after a first verb). Languages also have various ways of building conditional and passive constructions.

NOUN PHRASES

Vulgar Latin noun phrases balance a main noun or pronoun, descriptive elements like adjectives and determiner elements like articles, possessives and demonstratives. The Romance languages continue to reflect this conception of the noun phrase, but with differences among individual languages. In particular, some languages use possessives like *my* and *your* alongside the definite article, while other languages only allow one or the other.

Nouns, adjectives & articles

Romance nouns commonly occur together with an article and an adjective within a *noun phrase*. The types of articles, including occasions when a Romance noun takes no articles (zero articles), are introduced in an earlier chapter.

Most Romance adjectives follow the noun. The default placement of adjectives in Romance is to the right of the noun, while in English adjectives normally fall to the left of the noun: Spanish **ideas importantes**, Italian **idee importanti** for *important ideas*.

A handful of very common Romance adjectives regularly fall to the left of the noun instead: Spanish **buenas ideas**, Italian **buone idee** *good ideas*. A few adjectives have a very different meaning before and after the noun: Portuguese **grandes pessoas** *great people* versus **pessoas grandes** *big people*. Other adjectives are simply marked if placed to the left of the noun: Portuguese **importantes ideias** *important ideas* (versus the basic and expected **ideias importantes**).

Except for Romanian, languages place any articles to the left of the noun and adjective: French **l'idée importante** *the important idea*, **une idée importante** *an important idea*, **la grande idée** *the great idea*. In Romanian, the definite article attaches to the end of the noun: **un lucru important** *an important thing* but **lucrul important** *the important thing*. When a Romanian adjective precedes the noun and carries emphasis, the definite article attaches to it instead: **un bun samaritean** *a good Samaritan* versus **bunul samaritean** *the good Samaritan*.

*The noun phrase **l'antica bottega toscana** ("the old Tuscan shop")*
contains a definite article, an adjective before the noun and an adjective
after the noun. All agree with the noun's feminine gender.

Possessives, interrogatives & demonstratives

The Romance languages have a set of _demonstratives_ from Latin ***iste**, ***isse** and ***ille** or built from compounds containing ***iste** (near the speaker), ***isse/*ille** (distant from the speaker). Romance demonstratives function as deictic elements that point to the location of a specific noun: Portuguese **este homem**, Catalan **aquest home**, Sardinian **cust' ómine**, Romansh **quest um** *this man* (near me), versus

Portuguese **esse homem**, Catalan **aquell home**, Sardinian **cudd'**
ómine, Romansh **quel um** *that man*. Iberian languages have a third
location for nouns removed from both the speaker and the person
addressed: Portuguese **aquele homem**, Spanish **aquel hombre** *that*
man (distant from both of us).

French collapses the distance system, so the locations are no
longer distinct: **cet homme** translates to both *this man* and *that man*.
Speakers can clarify by marking the noun with **-ci** *here* or **-là** *there*:
cette homme-là explicitly means *that man*.

This next table gives masculine and feminine singular forms of
the demonstrative adjectives in representative languages.

	Spanish	Catalan	French	Sardinian	Romanian
this (near me)	este/esta	aquest/aquesta		custu/custa	acest/acesta
that (near you)	ese/esa		ce/cette		
that over there (away from us)	aquel/aquella	aquell/aquella		cuddu/cudda	acel/acela

In all languages, demonstrative adjectives replace the <u>article</u> in a
noun phrase, just as in English: Italian **questa idea**, Spanish **esta idea**
but not *la questa idea, *la esta idea for *this idea*.

The *interrogative adjectives* from Vulgar Latin *quale *which*,
quantu how much* and *quantos* how many* behave the same way:
Spanish **cuántas lenguas**, Portuguese **quantas línguas**, Italian **quante**
lingue, Romanian **câte limbi** *how many languages*. Again, these
modifiers take the place of an article but can be followed by another
adjective: Spanish **¿cuántas buenas ideas?** but not *las cuántas
buenas ideas for *how many good ideas?*

Romance languages also have a set of *possessive pronouns* that act
somewhat like <u>adjectives</u>, such as English *my* in *my book*. These usually
work like four-form adjectives, matching the masculine or feminine
<u>gender</u> and singular or plural <u>number</u> of the noun: French **mon mari**
my husband versus **ma femme** *my wife*. Spanish possessives do not
reflect gender in the basic word order, but can be placed after the
noun in marked orders, in which case they match the gender of the
noun: **mi amiga** *my [female] friend*, **mi amigo** *my [male] friend*, but **una**

amiga mía *a [female] friend of mine* versus **un amigo mío** *a [male] friend of mine.*

Romance languages are generally split between those that use the definite article with the possessive and those that do not: Spanish **mi idea** but not ***la mi idea** for *my idea* versus Italian **la mia idea** and not ***mia idea** or Catalan **la meva idea** but not just ***meva idea**. Portuguese makes allowances for both: **a minha ideia** or **minha ideia**. Romanian, which demands an article with the possessive, still attaches its definite article to the end of the noun: **prieten**, **prietenul** *friend*, *the friend*, **prietenul meu** *my friend*. In short, many Romance languages replace the article with the possessive, while others use both in tandem.

The following table contrasts the basic structure of noun phrases with possessives and determiners in two representative Romance languages.

structure	Vulgar Latin	Spanish	Italian	
article + noun	***illa idea**	**la idea**	**l'idea**	*the idea*
article + possessive + noun	***illa mea idea**		**la mia idea**	*my idea*
possessive + noun	***mea idea**	**mi idea**		
demonstrative + noun	***(eccu)ista idea**	**esta idea**	**quest'idea**	*this idea*

These examples intentionally oversimplify the matter. For instance, Italian does have possessives without articles when discussing close family: **mia madre** is used for *my mother*. French and Romansh parallel the ordering of Spanish, while Romanian, Sardinian and Catalan tend to stand behind the Italian structure.

When a possessive expression involves two <u>nouns</u> instead of a pronoun possessor, the Romance languages unanimously build a construction with **de** *of* plus a second noun after the main noun: ***illa casa de Anna**, Portuguese **a casa de Ana**, Romansh **la chasa da Anna** *Anna's house* (literally *the house of Anna*). Romanian can also put its <u>genitive</u>/<u>dative case</u> ending to work for this purpose: **casa prietenului meu** *my friend's house* (literally *the house my friend's*) versus **biroul de turism** *the office of tourism*. With <u>proper names</u>, Romanian speakers use a dative pronoun instead of **de**: **biroul lui Radu** *Radu's office* (literally *the office to-him Radu*) and not ***biroul de Radu**.

VERB PHRASES

Romance languages contain pronouns that revolve around the <u>verb</u>, so much so that their pronouns tend to act as <u>clitics</u> pronounced along with the verb as a single word. This section explores the basic order of these Romance pronouns around the verb.

Subject pronouns with verbs

Romance <u>verbs</u> have endings that carry information about the person and number of the <u>subject</u>: Western Romance ***fabulamus**, Portuguese **falamos** *we speak* has an ending **-amus** for the first person plural *we*. In Classical Latin, Vulgar Latin and most of the modern languages, the corresponding subject pronoun is routinely dropped: Vulgar Latin ***parabolant**, Catalan **parlen** and Italian **parlano** suffice for *they speak*. Speakers include the subject for clarity or emphasis: Vulgar Latin ***tu cantas**, Spanish **tú cantas** for *YOU sing*. So, the Romance languages have been described as languages with "optional" subjects or as <u>*pro-drop*</u> languages.

Subject pronoun dropping does not apply to the entire Romance world. Some languages developed into "keepers" instead of "droppers", particularly in France, Switzerland and the Italian Alps: French **je chante** and Romansh **jau chant** mean *I sing*, but not simply say ***chante** or ***chant**. These languages even expect <u>*expletives*</u> where pro-drop languages have no subject whatsoever (like with weather verbs): French **il pleut** *it rains* but not ***pleut** versus Italian **piove** *[it] rains* and not ***lui piove**.

Some subject-keeping languages have weak, unstressed subject pronouns that act as <u>clitics</u>: Emiliano-Romagnolo **a pèrle**, colloquial French **j'parle** for *I speak*. Rhaeto-Romance can but prefers not to attach subject clitics to the end of a verb: Romansh **chanta** in place of **jau chant** for *I sing*. In some of these languages, the subject may be _reinforced_ with non-clitic pronouns: Emiliano-Romagnolo **ei a pèrle** or **mé a pèrle**, colloquial French **moi j'parle** _me, I speak / I (emphatic) speak_.

The following table demonstrates how the various Romance languages drop or reinforce the subject pronoun.

language	dropped subject	retained subject	reinforced subject
Catalan	**canto**	**jo canto**	
French		**je chante**	**moi, je chante**
Romagnolo		**a cante**	**ei a cante**
Romansh	**(chanta)**	**jau chant**	**jau chanta**
Sardinian	**canto**	**deo canto**	
Romanian	**cânt**	**eu cânt**	

Direct or indirect object pronouns with verbs

Some verbs take a direct object, others an indirect object and still others take both. The selection of objects depends on the verb. When the object is referenced with a pronoun, Romance languages place direct or indirect object clitics next to the verb.

The Romance languages have a set of direct object pronouns that sit to the left of _transitive verbs_: Vulgar Latin ***illu vidio**, Sardinian **lu vido**, Italian **lo vedo**, Spanish **lo veo** _[I] see him_.

The Romance languages also have a set of indirect object pronouns that sit to the left of some ditransitive and _intransitive verbs_: Vulgar Latin ***illi do**, Sardinian **li do**, Italian **gli dò**, Spanish **le doy** _[I] give to him/her_. Outside of the third person, most Romance object pronouns no longer distinguish between direct and indirect objects.

	Vulgar Latin	Portuguese	Sardinian	Italian	
direct	***te vidio**	**te vejo**	**ti vido**	**ti vedo**	_I see you_
indirect	***ti promitto**	**te prometo**	**ti prominto**	**ti prometto**	_I promise to you_
direct	***illa vidio**	**a vejo**	**la vido**	**la vedo**	_I see her_
indirect	***illi promitto**	**lhe prometo**	**li prominto**	**gli prometto**	_I promise to her_

Only Romanian retains clearly distinct sets of indirect versus direct object pronouns: **îmi zice** *he says to me* versus **mă vede** *he sees me*, while Italian has **mi dice** and **mi vede**, failing to distinguish between <u>accusative</u> *me* and <u>dative</u> *to me*. For the examples above, Romanian has **te văd** *I see you* versus **îți promit** *I promise to you*.

Some languages can *<u>reinforce</u>* these object pronouns with <u>strong object pronouns</u>: Spanish **a ti te veo** *I see YOU*, Romanian **ție îți promit** *I promise TO YOU*, but not Italian ***te ti vedo** for *I see you*.

Both direct & indirect object pronouns with verbs

Many verb phrases contain both an <u>indirect</u> and <u>direct object</u>, like English *gives it to me*. In these situations, the Romance languages expect the sequence of indirect object + direct object before the verb: Spanish **te lo prometo**, French **je te le promets** *I promise it to you*. Again, the selection of objects depends on the <u>verb</u>.

In some languages, the shape of the indirect object pronoun changes before a direct object: Italian **te lo prometto** instead of the expected ***ti lo prometto** for *I promise it to you*. Other languages contract both pronouns when vowels make up the word boundary: Portuguese **to prometo** rather than ***te o prometto**, Romanian **ți-l promit** instead of ***îți îl promit**, Italian **glielo prometto** *I promise it to-her/him* and not ***gli lo prometto**.

With verbs in the <u>imperative mood</u>, object pronouns fall to the right of the verb instead of the left: French **dis-le-moi**, Romanian **spune-mi-l** *say it to me*. Some languages attach the pronouns directly to the verb: Spanish **dímelo**, Italian **dimmelo** *say it to me*.

These word orders apply to <u>reflexive object pronouns</u>, too: Spanish **se lo prometió**, Portuguese **so prometeu** *she promised it to herself*, and Italian **lavatevi**, French **lavez-vous** *wash yourselves*.

Galician and European Portuguese routinely place object pronouns after the verb: Portuguese **disseste-me** *you told me*, **chamo-me** *I call myself* (for *my name is*). Verbs with object pronouns that follow other material maintain the word order found in the rest of Romance: Portuguese **não me disseste** *you did not tell me* (introduced by a <u>negative</u> particle), **se me dissesses** *if you told me* (the beginning of a <u>hypothetical</u>).

Some languages make small adjustments with third-person pronouns. In French, the default order is <u>*reversed*</u> when both direct and indirect object are third person pronouns: **je le lui promets** rather than ***je lui le promets** for *I promise it to-him/her*. Italian makes the same change in word order, but only with the third person reflexive object: **lo si promette** *she promises it to herself* instead of ***se lo promette**, which is expected on analogy with **te lo prometto**. Spanish speakers replace the third-person indirect object **le** (singular) or **les** (plural) with **se** before a third-person direct object: **se lo prometo** and not ***les lo prometo** for *I promise it to them*.

Locatives & partitives

French, Italian, Catalan and a number of other Romance languages have small words that also act as <u>clitic pronouns</u>—Vulgar Latin ***ic** *there* and **en/ne** *some*: French **tu y vas**, Catalan **hi vas**, Italian **ci vai** *you go there*, and French **tu en veux**, Catalan **en vols**, Italian **ne vuoi** *you want some*, Italian **(tu) ne vuoi uno** *you want one of them*. The two pronouns have come to complement each other, the first meaning *to it/there* and the second *from it/there*: Italian **ne torno** *I return from-there* versus **ci torno** *I return to-there*.

In languages that have them, these <u>*locatives*</u> and <u>*partitives*</u> are placed alongside <u>direct</u> and <u>indirect object pronouns</u>. The examples below compare the placement of object pronouns in various Romance languages, including Spanish, which lacks partitive and locative pronouns.

	Spanish	French	Italian	
verb	**doy**	**je donne**	**do**	*I give*
verb + direct object	**lo doy**	**je le donne**	**lo do**	*I give it*
verb + direct + indirect object	**te lo doy**	**je te le donne**	**te lo do**	*I give it to you*
verb + partitive + indirect object	**te doy uno**	**je t'en donne un**	**te ne do uno**	*I give you one of them*

Impersonal verbs

Sometimes the apparent <u>subject</u> is less directly involved, and so acts as an experiencer rather than an agent. In these situations, Romance grammar treats the experiencer as an <u>indirect object</u> (a <u>dative</u> pronoun) and uses an *impersonal verb* that only appears in the third person: Spanish **me gusta** *I like [it]* (literally *[it] is-pleasing to-me*), Romanian **îmi trebuie** *I have to* (literally *[it] is-obligatory to-me*).

*Mayan ruins of Palenque in Mexico. Spanish **me gusta la arquitectura maya** ("Mayan architecture pleases me") uses a third-person verb form with an indirect object pronoun. English often uses a first-person subject instead ("I like Mayan architecture").*

If the thing experienced is made explicit, it will act as the grammatical subject and the verb will agree with its <u>number</u>: Spanish **me gustan** *I like them*. These grammatical subjects tend to follow the impersonal verb, demonstrating that the focus still rests on the experiencer: Spanish **le encantó la idea** *I loved the idea* but **me encantaron las ideas** *I loved the ideas*. The grammatical features of the object do not trigger changes in the verb: Spanish **les encantó la idea** but not ***les encantaron la idea** for *they loved the idea*. Impersonal verbs may also be followed by an <u>infinitive</u> (or the Romanian subjunctive):

Italian **mi piace lavorare** *I like to work* (literally *[it] pleases to-me to work*), Romanian **îmi place să lucrez** *I like to work* (literally *[it] pleases to-me that I work*).

Non-pro-drop Languages like French and Romansh require a subject, even in impersonal constructions. They expect dummy pronouns to fill the subject of an impersonal verb: French **il me plaît** *it pleases me* instead of just *****me plaît**.

Impersonal verbs are a very common way for Romance speakers to express experiences, including enjoyment and obligation.

language	impersonal verb	structure	
Italian	**piace**	**mi piace fare**	*I like to do*
Occitan	**cal**	**me cal far**	*I have to do*
Spanish	**gusta**	**me gusta hacer**	*I like to do*
French	**il faut**	**il me faut faire**	*I have to do*

BASIC SENTENCES

Classical Latin had a fairly free *word order*: Latin **Brutus murum construit** (SOV), **Brutus construit murum** (SVO), **murum construit Brutus** (OVS), **construit Brutus murum** (VSO), **construit murum Brutus** (VOS), **murum Brutus construit** (OSV) are all possible (but not equally preferred) configurations for *Brutus builds [a] wall*. The Romance languages have developed more precise expectations of where words fall within a sentence. This introduction surveys the order within affirmations, negations and questions with a single verb. It will avoid the details of the word order within verb phrases and noun phrases.

Affirmative sentences

The basic word order of a Romance sentence is subject, verb, object: Vulgar Latin *****ego fabulo latinu**, Spanish **yo hablo latín**, Galician **eu falo latín** (subject + verb + object) *I speak Latin*. Such sentences typically contain a main verb in the indicative mood. As discussed elsewhere, most Romance languages routinely drop subject pronouns (<u>pro-drop</u>), leaving many sentences with only a <u>verb</u> and its <u>objects</u>: Vulgar Latin **fabulo latinu**, Spanish **hablo latín**, Galician **falo latín** (verb + object) *I speak Latin*.

Direct and <u>indirect object pronouns</u> fall to the left of the verb instead of the right, leaving the word order subject + object + verb, where "object" means object pronouns: Vulgar Latin ***(ego) illu fabulo***, Spanish **(yo) lo hablo** *I speak it*.

Negative sentences

The basic word order of affirmative sentences holds for <u>*negative*</u> sentences, but languages generally add a negative particle ***non** before the verb: Vulgar Latin ***non fabulo latinu**, Spanish ***no hablo latín** I do not speak Latin*. Since object pronouns are treated as a unit with the verb, the negative precedes them, too: Portuguese **não to prometo**, Romanian **nu ți-l promit** *I do not promise it to you*.

Some languages instead add a reinforcing negative after the verb along with ***ne** before the verb: Romansh **jau na sai betg**, French **je ne sais pas** *I do not know*. Modern French and Swiss Romance view the reinforcing negation as the main negative particle, and often delete the original Latin negative particle: colloquial French **je sais pas** or **j'sais pas** *I don't know*. This switch is complete in Occitan, where **pas** is left as the only negation: **sabi pas** *I don't know*.

Romance languages have other negative words like French **jamais** *never* or Sardinian **nudda** *nothing*. Languages can add these negative words to build sentences with multiple negations, including double or triple negatives: Spanish **no me dice nada** *[she] doesn't tell me anything* (literally *[she] doesn't tell me nothing*) or French **elle n'oublie jamais rien** *she never forgets anything* (*she doesn't forget never nothing*).

The Romance syntax tables at the end of this book compare negations across representative languages.

Yes-no questions

Yes-no questions lack a question word like *who* or *what*. All languages allow questions to remain close to the structure of affirmative sentences in Romance, typically with rising intonation near the end: Catalan **(tu) fas un projecte?**, French **tu fais un projet ?**, Romanian **(tu) faci un proiect?** *are you doing a project?* (literally *you do a project?*).

Languages can also *move* the subject after the verb to mark interrogative word order: Catalan **tu ho fas** *you do it* but **ho fas tu?** *do you do it?*, Romanian **eu vin** *I come* but **nu vin eu?** *do I not come?* This subject movement is not limited to questions in most languages, so it need not be seen only as a question-marking strategy: Spanish **si lo sabes tú** *if you know it* (literally *if it know you*). Sardinian uses a question marker **a** at the beginning of the sentence, with the subject placed after the verb: **(tue) nde cheres** *you want some* is questioned as **a nde cheres (tue)?** *do you want some?* (where **tue** is typically dropped and **nde** is the partitive).

Subject movement is avoided in a number of languages and dialects: Caribbean Spanish **¿tú habla latín?** *do you speak Latin?*, or colloquial French **tu parles latin ?** versus the more formal or literary French **parles-tu latin ?** for *do you speak Latin?* When the subject is a noun instead of a pronoun, subject-moving registers of French leave the noun and add a pronoun to the right of the verb: **Jean vient-il ?** *is John coming?* instead of **vient-Jean?* When the French verb ends in a vowel, **-t-** is added between the verb and the subject pronoun: **Jean parle-t-il latin ?** instead of **Jean parle-il latin ?* for *does John speak Latin?*

Some languages introduce a question with a short question phrase, which allows the main sentence to retain its basic order: European Portuguese **(tu) o fazes** becomes **é que (tu) o fazes?**, Dominican Spanish **(tú) lo hace** becomes **¿e que (tú) lo hace?**, and French **tu le fais** becomes **est-ce que tu le fais ?** *are you doing it?* (literally *is it that you do it?*). In French, this is a very standard tactic for building questions: **est-ce que tu parles latin ?** *do you speak Latin?*

The Romance syntax tables at the end of this book compare basic yes-no questions across representative languages.

Questions with question words

Romance languages contain *interrogatives* like *quid *what* and interrogative adverbs like *quando *when*. As in English, these interrogatives are *moved* to the beginning of a sentence when they are used to ask a question: colloquial French **quoi tu vois ?**, European Portuguese **que vês?**, Romanian **ce vezi?** *what [do] you see?* or Spanish **¿cuándo vienes?**, Romanian **când vii** *when are you coming?* This movement is hidden when the question word is the subject: French **qui est venu ?** *who has come?* alongside **il est venu** *he has come*, or Spanish **¿qué pasó?** *what happened?* alongside **eso pasó** *that happened*.

Some languages can leave the question word in its expected position, but this order is marked: French **tu veux X** *you want X*, **tu veux quoi ?** *you want what?*

If the subject is not the question word, languages can move the subject to the right of the verb, just as in yes-no questions: Romansh **tge fas ti?**, Catalan **què fas tu?**, Italian **che fai tu?**, Spanish **¿qué haces tú?**, Romanian **ce faci tu?** *what are you doing?* (literally *what do you?*). This is a common way to ask a question in Romance, and is found both with and without the subject: Romanian **ce faci?**, Spanish **¿qué haces?**, Sardinian **ite faghes?** *what are you doing?* Some languages, including colloquial French and Caribbean Spanish, avoid moving the subject: nonstandard French **quoi tu dis ?**, Caribbean Spanish **¿qué tú diceh?** for *what do you say / are you saying?*

Languages that can introduce a question with *est quod place the interrogative before the phrase and the rest of the sentence after: European Portuguese **que é que (tu) fazes?** and French **qu'est-ce que tu fais ?** *what are you doing?* (literally *what is it that you do?*), or French **qui est-ce que tu vois ?** *who is it that you see?* This is the default question structure in French, but not in other languages.

The Romance syntax tables at the end of this book compare questions using question words in representative languages.

*A **métro de Paris** signpost in the Art Nouveau style. The question **quelle ligne?** ("which line?") employs the Latin question word **qualem** ("which") .*

Imperative sentences

Romance commands are straightforward structures. The basic <u>word order</u> of affirmative sentences is maintained, but the tendency to drop the subject (<u>pro-drop</u>) becomes much stronger: European Portuguese **tu falas latim** *you speak Latin* relates to the <u>imperative</u> **fala latim!** *speak Latin!* When <u>object pronouns</u> occur with an imperative verb, they turn to follow the verb: Italian **me lo dici** *you say it to me* but **dimmelo!** *say it to me!*

The Romance languages make routine use of the <u>subjunctive</u> to soften an imperative, as well as to form negative and formal commands.

COMPOUND & OTHER SENTENCES

Latin and Romance have a variety of sentences beyond the basic <u>affirmative</u>, <u>negative</u> and <u>interrogative</u> types. This section explores more types of sentences that Romance languages can build, with a focus on *compound sentences*, which contain multiple verbs.

Dependent clauses: finite second verbs

The Romance languages build a sentence around a _finite verb_—a <u>verb</u> <u>stem</u> with endings carrying information about <u>person</u>, <u>number</u>, <u>tense</u>, <u>aspect</u> and <u>mood</u>. In simple sentences, each finite verb falls in a separate sentence, and each sentence contains one finite verb. However, the Romance languages can embed one finite sentence into another by linking the two with ***quod** _that_: Vulgar Latin ***scio quod me amas**, Sardinian **isco chi mi amas** _I know that you love me._

The short particle that links the two finite verbs differs from language to language, but representative spellings include Italian **che** and Spanish **que**. The use of this particle remains consistent throughout Romance: Spanish **dicen que cantas bien**, Galician **din que cantas ben**, Catalan **diuen que cantes bé** French **ils disent que tu chantes bien**, Romansh **els dian che ti chantas bain** _they say that you sing well._

A significant exception to this tendency to append a second finite verb with ***quod** is Romanian preference for **să** plus a verb in the <u>subjunctive</u>. Romanian speakers link the first verb to the second with **să**: **îmi trebuie să merg** _it is necessary that I go._ Other languages expect the two verbs to refer to grammatically distinct <u>subjects</u>: Spanish does not have ***puede que canta**, Italian lacks ***può che canta**, French does not build ***il peut qu'il chante** just as English lacks _*he can that he sings_. Romanian, like other Balkan languages, does not have this limitaton: **poate să cânte** _he can sing_ (literally _[he] can that [he] sings_).

The <u>tense</u> and <u>mood</u> of the second verb found after ***quod** depends on the tense and meaning of the first. In particular, the meaning of the first verb can trigger the use of the subjunctive in the post-***quod** verb: indicative in Spanish **sabemos que canta bien** _we know that she sings well_ versus subjunctive **esperamos que cante bien** _we hope that she sing well_. Romanian is unique in that any verb following **să** takes the subjunctive mood, regardless of the first verb's meaning: **poate să cânte** but not ***poate să cântă**.

The syntax tables at the end of this book compare sentences with second verbs introduced by ***quod** across the Romance languages.

Infinitives as second verbs

Vulgar Latin and the modern Romance languages have an infinitive form of the verb that carries the meaning of a verb but without the grammatical information found in finite verbs: Vulgar Latin **cantare**, Spanish **cantar**, Romansh **chantar**, Corsican **cantà**, Sardinian **cantare** *to sing*. In many cases, rather than packing a second verb into a dependent clause marked by *quod, the second verb may directly follow the first verb as an infinitive: Vulgar Latin *potet cantare, Spanish **puede cantar**, French **il peut chanter**, Sardinian **podet cantare** *he can sing*.

A number of Romance verbs are normally followed by an infinitive. In most cases, the finite verb and the infinitve refer to the exact same subject: Portuguese **ele canta** *he sings*, **ele pode** *he can*, **ele pode cantar** *he can sing*. Structures like Vulgar Latin *queres cantare *you want to sing* come to mean only *you want yourself to sing*, not *you want him to sing* or *you want me to sing*. Verbs of perception provide a clear exception, but these must take an object pronoun to denote the apparent subject of the infinitive: Italian **la vedo cantare** *I see her sing* alongside the finite Italian **vedo che canta** *I see that she sings*. Romance verbs of mood (modals) and perception as well as prepositional verbs are followed by an infinitive.

Uniquely, the Romanian languages prefer second finite clauses introduced by **să** to an infinitive. Romanian does retain infinitives, but their use is reduced: **poate să cânte** *[he] can that [he] sings* is preferred to **poate cânta** *[he] can sing*.

The Romance syntax tables at the end of this book contain examples of infinitive second verbs in the Romance languages.

Hypothetical sentences

Romance languages differ between East and West in how they build *hypothetical* if...then statements. Most languages introduce the *if*-statement with an imperfect subjunctive verb: Italian **se potessi...**, Portuguese **se pudesse** *if I could...*. The *then*-statement contains a conditional verb in much of Romance: Italian **canterei bene**, Portuguese **cantaria bem** *I would sing well*. Modern French prefers an imperfect indicative in the *if*-statement instead: literary/archaic French

si je pusse, je chanterais bien versus conversational French **si je pouvais, je chanterais bien** *if I could, I would sing well.*

Romanian uses the <u>helping verb</u> ***abere** *to have* in both halves of the hypothetical: **dacă aș putea** *if I could* (literally *if I would be able*), **dacă aș putea aș cânta bine** *if I could I would sing well.* This symmetry (conditional + conditional) is heard elsewhere in Romance hypotheticals, including in nonstandard dialects or registers: Romansh **sche jau pudess, jau chantass bain** *if I would be able, I would sing well* (where the conditional has endings similar to the imperfect subjunctive in other Romance languages), colloquial French **si je pourrais, je chanterais bien** *if I would be able, I would sing well.*

Passive sentences

As discussed in the introduction to ***essere** and ***abere**, Romance languages can form a *passive* with ***essere** and a <u>past participle</u>: Vulgar Latin ***illu libru est scriptu**, Italian **il libro è scritto**, Portuguese **o livro é escrito** *the book is written.* Romansh prefers ***venire** and a past participle instead: **il cudesch vegn scrit** *the book is written* (literally *the book comes written*). Languages can resurface the active <u>subject</u> with a <u>prepositional phrase</u>: Portuguese **é escrito por João**, Romansh **i vegn scrit da Gion** *it is written by John.*

Some languages prefer to use a general third-person pronoun with an active verb to express the passive: French **on parle latin** roughly *we speak / one speaks Latin* and not ***latin est parlé** for *Latin is spoken*, or Romansh **ins scriva** *one writes* alongside **i vegn scrit** for *it is written.* Along these lines, some languages can use a third person-plural in a similar sense: Spanish **¿qué dijeron?** *what did they say?* for *what was said?*

Romance speakers regularly use a third-person <u>reflexive verb</u> for the passive. This way of forming the passive dominates the Romance world. In this construction, the pronoun **se** is used with the verb: Italian **si scrive**, Catalan **s'escriu**, Spanish **se escribe**, Romanian **se scrie** for *it is written.* The number of the verb matches the number of the passive subject: Spanish **el verbo se escribe** versus **los verbos se escriben**, Sardinian **su verbu s'iscriet** versus **sos verbos s'iscrient**, Romanian **verbul se scrie** but **verbele se scriu** for *the verb is written* versus *the verbs are written*. Unlike ***essere** with a past participle, the original active subject is left out: Spanish ***se escribe por Juan**, Italian ***si scrive da Giovanni** do not get used for *it is written by John*.

The **Pont du Gard** *near Nîmes. Late Latin verbs took passive endings, as in ***aquaeductus bastiatur** (aqueduct build-passive). Romance developed new structures like Occitan **l'aqüeducte es bastit** ("the aqueduct is built") or **l'aqüeducte se bastís** ("the aqueduct builds itself").*

The table below compares various Romance ways of expressing the passive voice.

passive structure	Latin example	literal translation	distribution
(active endings)	*cantat	*sings*	all Romance languages
passive endings	*cantatur	*is-sung*	only in Latin
reflexive	*se cantat	*sings itself*	nearly every language
be + past participle	*est cantatu	*is sung*	many languages
generic third-person pronoun	*omo/unus cantat	*man/one sings*	French, Romansh; weakly in Catalan, Spanish
third-person plural	*cantant	*they sing*	all languages

Grammar Tables

NOUNS

Masculine nouns in -u

*lupu\n wolf	nominative singular	accusative singular	dative singular	nominative singular	accusative singular	dative singular
Latin	lúpus	lúpum	lúpo	lúpi	lúpos	lúpis
Portuguese		lobo			lobos	
Asturian		llobu			llobos	
Spanish		lobo			lobos	
Catalan		llop			llops	
Occitan		lop			lops	
Old French	loups	loup		loup	loups	
French		loup			loups	
Romansh		luf			lufs	
Sardinian		lupu			lupos	
Italian		lupo		lupi		
Romanian		lup	lup	lupi		lupi

- All languages. The modern languages collapse or lose the formal case distinctions of Latin nouns. The table shows the Latin cases from which modern *masculine noun* forms are derived, and does not reflect their current grammatical use.

- Catalan, Occitan, French, Rhaeto-Romansh, Romanian. A number of languages lose the characteristic -o/-u gender marker, so that many of their masculine nouns end in a consonant: Vulgar Latin *factu becomes Catalan fet, French fait and Romanian fapt *fact*.

- All languages. A few nouns in -o/-u are feminine: Italian mano, Portuguese mão. This retention is obscured in languages that have lost the gender marker: Catalan mà, French main *hand*.

- Romanian. Romanian nouns distinguish two cases: nominative/accusative versus genitive/dative.

Feminine nouns in -a

*lista *list*	nominative singular	accusative singular	dative singular	nominative plural	accusative plural	dative plural
Latin	*lísta	*lístam	*lístae	*lístae	*lístas	*lístis
Portuguese		lista			listas	
Asturian		llista			llistas	
Spanish		lista			listas	
Catalan		llista			llistes	
Occitan		lista			listas	
Old French	*liste	*liste		*listes	*listes	
French		liste			listes	
Romansh		glista			glistas	
Sardinian		lista			listas	
Italian		lista		liste		
Romanian		listă	liste	liste		liste

- All languages. The example ***lista** was borrowed into the Romance languages, not inherited from Classical Latin. However, this modern noun nicely showcases the regular feminine endings across the family. Along with such garden-variety _feminine nouns_, a small set of <u>masculine nouns</u> also ends in **-a**: ***artista** and ***problema** are masculine.

- Occitan. Latin **-a** changes to **-o** in some dialects: Vulgar Latin ***vita** _life_ becomes Provençal **vido**. This change is not always reflected in the spelling: standard Occitan **vida**.

- French. Latin **-a** changes to a silent **-e** and Latin plural **-as** changes to a silent **-es**.

- Romanian. Some feminine nouns in **-ă** have a <u>plural</u> in **-i** instead. The <u>genitive</u>/dative singular of nouns in **-ă** matches the plural: **cunună** _wreath_ has the genitive/dative **cununi** and the plural **cununi**.

Neuter nouns in -u

*ferru *iron*	nominative singular	accusative singular	dative singular	nominative plural	accusative plural	dative plural
Latin	**férrum**	**férrum**	**férro**	**férra**	**férra**	**férris**
Portuguese		**ferro**			**ferros**	
Asturian		**fierro**			**fierros**	
Spanish		**hierro**			**hierros**	
Catalan		**ferro**			**ferros**	
Occitan		**fèrre**			**fèrres**	
Old French	**fers**	**fer**		**fer**	**fers**	
French		**fer**			**fers**	
Romansh		**fier**			**fiers**	
Sardinian		**ferru**			**ferros**	
Italian		**ferro**		**ferra**		
Romanian		**fier**	**fier**	**fiare**		**fiare**

- All languages. Romance languages on the whole treat Latin <u>neuter nouns</u> like <u>masculine nouns</u>. Portuguese, Spanish, Catalan, Occitan, French, Italian and most other languages distinguish masculine and <u>feminine nouns</u>.

- Asturian. This "neuter" ending marks a <u>collective</u> noun: **fierro** (with "neuter" **-o**) versus **fierru** (with masculine **-u**).

- Romansh, Italian. These languages do not possess a strict set of neuter nouns. The neuter is repurposed for grouped or paired nouns that are masculine when ungrouped: **ferro** (singular), **ferra** (collective), **ferri** (plural). Some regional languages do retain neuter and masculine nouns: Neapolitan distinguishes the neuter **(f)fierro** from masculine **fierro**.

- Romanian. These neuter nouns resemble masculine nouns in the singular and feminine nouns in the <u>plural</u>. However, the plural ending **-uri** is unique to neuter nouns: speakers may say **fieruri** instead of **fiare**.

Nouns of any gender in -e

*auctore _author_	nominative singular	accusative singular	dative singular	nominative plural	accusative plural	dative plural
Latin	auctor	auctorem	auctori	auctores	auctores	auctoribus
Portuguese		autor			autores	
Asturian		autor			autores	
Spanish		autor			autores	
Catalan		autor			autors	
Occitan		autor			autors	
Old French	autheurs	autheur		autheur	autheurs	
French		auteur			auteurs	
Romansh		autur			auturs	
Sardinian		autore			autores	
Italian		autore			autori	
Romanian		autor	autor		autori	autori

- All languages. <u>Nouns</u> in **-e** may belong to either <u>gender</u>.

- Italian, Romanian. The <u>plural</u> ends in **-i** as with <u>masculine nouns</u>. This holds for the Romanian <u>genitive</u>/dative plural as well.

Common feminine endings: -ione and -itate

*actione *action*	nominative singular	accusative singular	dative singular	nominative plural	accusative plural	dative plural
Latin	áctio	actiónem	actióni	actiónes	actiónes	actiónibus
Old Portuguese		acçõ			acções	
Portuguese		ação			ações	
Asturian		acción			acciones	
Spanish		acción			acciones	
Catalan		acció			accións	
Occitan		accion			accions	
French		action			actions	
Romansh		acziun			acziuns	
Sardinian		atzione			atziones	
Italian		azione			azioni	
Romanian		acțiune	acțiuni		acțiuni	acțiuni

*activitate *activity*	nominative singular	accusative singular	dative singular	nominative plural	accusative plural	dative plural
Latin	actívitas	activitátem	activitáti	activitátes	activitátes	activitátibus
Old Portuguese		actividade			actividades	
Portuguese		atividade			atividades	
Asturian		actividad			actividades	
Spanish		actividad			actividades	
Catalan		activitat			activitats	
Occitan		activitat			activitats	
French		activité			activités	
Romansh		activitad			activitads	
Sardinian		atividade			atividades	
Italian		attività			attività	
Romanian		activitate	activități		activități	activități

ARTICLES

Masculine definite article

*illu lupu *the wolf*	nominative singular	accusative singular	dative singular	nominative plural	accusative plural	dative plural
Latin	ílle	íllum	illíus	ílli	íllos	illórum
Portuguese		o lobo			os lobos	
Asturian		el llobu			los llobos	
Spanish		el lobo			los lobos	
Catalan		el llop			els llops	
Occitan		lo lop			los lops	
Old French	li loups	le loup		li loup	les loups	
French		le loup			les loups	
Romansh		il luf			ils lufs	
Sardinian		su lupu			sos lupos	
Italian		il lupo		i lupi		
Romanian		lupul	lupului	lupii		lupilor

- Asturian, Catalan, Occitan, French, Romansh, Italian. The singular *definite article* is reduced to l' before a vowel: Catalan l'amic, Italian l'amico *the friend*.

- Italian. The singular and plural articles are l' and gli before vowels: l'atto, gli atti *the act, the acts*. The singular definite article is lo before z- or consonant clusters beginning in s-: lo zio *the uncle*.

- Sardinian, Balearic Catalan. The definite article comes from Vulgar Latin *issu, not *illu. This gives the characteristic s- versus the l- of most Romance definite articles. The singular article is reduced to s' before a vowel: Sardinian s'ómine *the man*.

- Romanian. Masculine nouns in -e take the articles -le and -elui in the singular instead: câine, câinele, cânelui, câinii, câinilor *dog, the dog, of the dog, the dogs, of the dogs*.

Masculine indefinite article

*unu lupu *a wolf*	nominative singular	accusative singular	dative singular	nominative plural	accusative plural	dative plural
Latin	únus	únum	uníus	úni	únos	unórum
Portuguese		um lobo			uns lobos	
Asturian		un llobu			unos llobos	
Spanish		un lobo			unos lobos	
Catalan		un llop			uns llops	
Occitan		un lop			unis lops	
Old French	uns loups	un loup		un loup	uns loups	
French		un loup			des loups	
Romansh		in luf			lufs	
Sardinian		unu lupu			unos lupos	
Italian		un lupo		uni lupi		
Romanian		un lup	unui lup	unii lupi		unor lupi

- All languages. The plural _indefinite article_ denotes a group or portion, similar to English *some*. Most of the Romance languages (apart from French) can simply use the <u>bare noun</u> in the plural.

- Old French, French. The plural indefinite article is lost in later Old French. Modern French uses the partitive **des**: **un loup, des loups** *a wolf, (some) wolves*.

- Occitan. The _partitive_ **de** is the preferred plural indefinite article: **un lop, de lops** *a wolf, wolves*.

- Sardinian. The singular article is reduced to **un'** before a vowel: **un'ómine** *a man*.

- Italian. The singular indefinite article is **uno** before **z-** or a consonant cluster beginning in **s-**: **uno spagnolo**. Also, like French and Occitan, Italian can use a partitive (masculine **dei**, feminine **delle**): **un lupo, dei lupi** *a wolf, some wolves*.

- Romansh. Speakers abandon the indefinite article in the plural: **in luf, lufs** *a wolf, wolves*.

Feminine definite article

*illa lista / the list	nominative singular	accusative singular	dative singular	nominative plural	accusative plural	dative plural
Latin	ílla	íllam	illíus	íllae	íllas	illárum
Portuguese		a lista			as listas	
Asturian		la llista			les llistes	
Spanish		la lista			las listas	
Catalan		la llista			les llistes	
Occitan		la lista			las listas	
Old French	*la liste	*la liste		*les listes	*les listes	
French		la liste			les listes	
Romansh		la glista			las glistas	
Sardinian		sa lista			sas listas	
Italian		la lista		le liste		
Romanian		lista	listei	listele		listelor

- All languages. The example ***illa lista** represents a borrowing into the Romance languages, not a term inherited from Classical Latin. However, this modern noun nicely showcases the regular feminine endings across the family.

- Asturian, Catalan, Occitan, French, Romansh, Italian. The singular _definite article_ is reduced to **l'** before a vowel: Catalan **l'aigua**, Emiliano-Romagnolo **l'aqua** _the water_.

- Sardinian, Balearic Catalan. The singular article is inherited from ***issa**, not ***illa**. It gets reduced to **s'** before a vowel: Sardinian **s'abba**, Balearic **s'aigua** _the water_.

- Romanian. The definite article is attached after the <u>noun</u> endings: **cunună, cununi, cununa, cununile** _wreath, wreaths, the wreath, the wreaths_.

Feminine indefinite article

*una lista *a list*	nominative singular	accusative singular	dative singular	nominative plural	accusative plural	dative plural
Latin	úna	únam	uníus	únae	únas	unárum
Portuguese		uma lista			umas listas	
Asturian		una llista			unes llistes	
Spanish		una lista			unas listas	
Catalan		una llista			unes llistes	
Occitan		una lista			unes listas	
Old French	*une liste	*une liste		*unes listes	*unes listes	
French		une liste			des listes	
Romansh		ina glista			glistas	
Sardinian		una lista			unas listas	
Italian		una lista		une liste		
Romanian		o listă	unei liste	unele liste		unor liste

- All languages. General remarks about the masculine _indefinite article_ apply.

- Romansh, Sardinian, Italian. The feminine article is reduced before a <u>noun</u> beginning in a vowel: Italian **un'amica**, Romansh **in'amia** *a [female] friend*.

Neuter definite article

*illu ferru *the iron*	nominative singular	accusative singular	dative singular	nominative plural	accusative plural	dative plural
Latin	**íllud**	**íllum**	**illíus**	**ílla**	**íllas**	**illórum**
Asturian		**lo**				
Spanish		**lo**				
Romansh		**il fier**			**la fiera**	
Italian		**il ferro**		**le ferra**		
Romanian		**fierul**	**fierului**	**fiarele**		**fiarelor**

- All languages. The modern languages treat Latin neuter nouns like masculine nouns. Earlier remarks about <u>neuter nouns</u> still apply.

- Asturian, Spanish. Neuter forms occur only in the singular—their plurals are masculine. The neuter *definite article* is commonly used with masculine adjectives: Spanish **lo importante** *the important (thing)*, Asturian **lo bono** *the good (thing)*. The parallel construction in most Romance languages contains a masculine article.

- Rhaeto-Romansh, Italian. Neuter forms are used for grouped or paired nouns (<u>collective neuters</u>). These nouns often have a parallel masculine plural: **il braccio, le braccia, i bracci** *the arm, the (pair of) arms, the (multiple ungrouped) arms* versus **l'uovo, le uova** (rather than ***gli uovi**) *the egg, the eggs*.

- Romanian. Neuter nouns and articles are treated like masculine forms in the singular and feminine forms in the plural.

Neuter indefinite article

*unu ferru *an iron*	nominative singular	accusative singular	dative singular	nominative plural	accusative plural	dative plural
Latin	**únum**	**únum**	**uníus**	**úna**	**úna**	**unórum**
Romanian		**un fier**	**unui fier**	**unele fiare**		**unelor fiare**

- All languages. General remarks about the masculine *indefinite article* apply.

PERSONAL PRONOUNS

Subject pronouns

Latin	égo	tu	ílle	ílla	nos	vos	íllos	íllas
Portuguese	eu	tu	ele	ela	nós	vós	eles	elas
Galician	eu	ti	ele	ela	nós/ nosoutros	vós/ vosoutros	eles	elas
Spanish	yo	tú	él	ella	nosotros	vosotros	ellos	ellas
Catalan	jo	tu	ell	ella	nosaltres	vosaltres	ells	elles
Occitan	ieu	tu	el	ela	nosautres	vosautres	eles	elas
French	je	tu	il	elle	nous	vous	ils	elles
Romansh	jau	ti	el	ella	nus	vus	els	ellas
Sardinian	deo	tue	isse	issa	nois	vois	issos	issas
Italian	io	tu	lui	lei	noi	voi	loro	loro
Romanian	eu	tu	el	ea	noi	voi	ei	ele
	I	*you*	*he*	*she*	*we*	*all of you*	*they*	*they (all fem.)*

- All languages. <u>*Subject pronouns*</u> are optional in most Romance languages: **finiscono** or **loro finiscono** *they finish*. Rhaeto-Romansh and the French langues d'oïl are the major exceptions: French **ils finissent** but not just **finissent**.

- All languages. The third-person masculine pronouns double as the gender-neutral or <u>default</u> pronouns. Many languages have a <u>neuter</u> subject pronoun: Spanish **ello**, French **ça**, Italian **ciò** *it*. <u>Demonstratives</u> also see wide use in these instances: Portuguese **isso é...** *that is...*, Romanian **asta este...** *this is...*

- Portuguese. Speakers also use a <u>polite</u> second-person pronoun **você** and the very formal **o senhor** (to a male) and **a senhora** (to a female). All of these pronouns have a corresponding plural: **vocês, os senhores, as senhoras**. Some Brazilian varieties have lost both **tu** and **vós**. European speakers have generally lost **vós**.

- Galician, Spanish, Catalan, Sardinian, Italian. These languages also have a formal or polite second-person pronoun: Galician **vostede**, Spanish **usted**, Catalan **vostè**, Sardinian **vosté**. All have corresponding plural forms: **vostedes**, **ustedes**, **vostés**. Italian has a similar system, but uses **Lei** in the singular and **Loro** in the plural. These polite pronouns are treated grammatically like third-person pronouns.

- Galician, Spanish, Catalan, Occitan. The first-person plural is built from Latin ***nos altros** (masculine) and ***nos altras** (feminine), both meaning *we others*. The Catalan form no longer distinguishes between masculine and feminine, but Spanish and Occitan do.

- Occitan, French, Romansh. Speakers also use the second-person plural to address a single person politely: French **vous êtes** *you are (singular) / all of you are*. In Occitan, the polite pronoun is **vos**, not **vosautres/vosautras**.

- Romansh. Speakers may instead attach reduced forms of these pronouns to the end of a verb: **jau chant** or **chanta** *I sing*. Also, the third-person pronoun **i** acts as a <u>dummy pronoun</u> in the singular and as a generic masculine or feminine third-person pronoun.

- Sardinian. Speakers use forms of Latin **ipse** instead of **ille** for the third-person singular and plural pronouns.

- Italian. Speakers use words derived from Latin **illi** and **illorum** for the third-person singular and plural pronouns. Singular variants **egli** and **ella** (from the nominative case **ille** and **illa**) are restricted to formal writing and discourse.

- Romanian. Speakers also use an equalizing second-person pronoun **mata** and the formal or polite pronoun **dumneata**. The polite plural is **dumneavoastră**. Romanian also has the semiformal third-person pronouns **dânsul** *he*, **dânsa** *she*, **dânşii** *they* and **dânsele** *they*, along with the very formal **dumnealui** (singular) and **dumneaei** (plural).

Prepositional & strong object pronouns

Latin	me/ míhi	te/ tíbi	íllum	íllam	nos	vos	íllos	íllas	se/ síbi
Portuguese	mim	ti	ele	ela	nós	vós	eles	elas	si
Galician	min	ti	el	ela	nós	vós	eles	elas	si
Spanish	mí	ti	él	ella	nosotros	vosotros	ellos	ellas	sí
Catalan	mi	ti	ell	ella	nosaltres	vosaltres	ells	elles	si
Occitan	ieu	tu	el	ela	nosautres	vosautres	eles	elas	se
French	moi	toi	lui	elle	nous	vous	eux	elles	soi
Romansh	mai	tai	el	ella	nus	vus	els	ellas	sai
Sardinian	a mie	a tie	issu	issa	nois	vois	issos	issas	se
Italian	me	te	lui	lei	noi	voi	loro	loro	se
Romanian	mine	tine	el	ea	noi	voi	ei	ele	sine
	me	*you*	*him*	*her*	*us*	*all of you*	*them*	*them (all fem.)*	*him/herself, themselves*

- All languages. These pronouns act as an mphasized <u>direct object</u>, generally the object of a <u>preposition</u>: Romanian **pentru mine**, French **pour moi**, Italian **per me** *for me*.

- Portuguese, Galician, Spanish, Sardinian. In the Western Iberian languages and Sardinian, pronouns combine with the Latin preposition **cu(n)* *with*: Spanish **conmigo**, Portuguese **comigo**, Sardinian **cun megus** *with me*.

- French. Speakers use these pronouns on their own or to <u>reinforce</u> another pronoun: **moi?** *me?*, **moi, je suis...** *I am...*

Direct object pronouns

Latin	me	te	íllum	íllam	nos	vos	íllos	íllas	se/ síbi
Portuguese	me	te	o	a	nos	vos	os	as	se
Galician	me	te	o	a	nos	vos	os	as	se
Spanish	me	te	lo	la	nos	os	los	las	se
Catalan	me	te	lo	la	nos	vos	los	les	se
Occitan	me	te	lo	la	nos	vos	los	las	se
French	me	te	le	la	nous	vous	les	les	se
Romansh	ma	ta	al	la	ans	as	als	las	sa
Sardinian	mi	ti	lu	la	nos	vos	los	las	si
Italian	mi	ti	lo	la	ci	vi	li	le	si
Romanian	mă	te	îl	o	ne	vă	îi	le	se
	me	*you*	*him*	*her*	*us*	*all of you*	*them*	*them (all fem.)*	*him/herself, themselves*

- All languages. These unstressed _direct bject pronouns_ act as the object of a <u>verb</u>: Italian **ti vedono**, Spanish **te ven**, Romanian **te văd** all mean *(they) see you*. Most languages treat unreferenced objects as <u>masculine</u>, but Catalan and Occitan have a <u>neuter</u> object pronoun from Latin **hoc**: Occitan **o vesi**, Catalan **ho veig** *I see it*.

- All languages. Object pronouns follow an imperative verb: French **lavez-vous**, Italian **lavatevi** *wash yourselves*. Some Western Iberian languages can place the object pronoun after an <u>indicative</u> verb: Old Spanish **véote**, Portuguese **vejo-te**, Galician **véxote** *I see you*.

- Romansh. Speakers can instead use the stressed object pronouns with a verb: **els ta vesan** or **els vesan tai** *they see you*.

- Catalan, Occitan, French, Romansh, Sardinian, Italian, Romanian. Object pronouns ending in a vowel contract with verbs that begin with a vowel: Catalan **l'estimen**, Sardinian **l'istimant** *(they) love her*. Catalan object pronouns also have a separate form before a consonant: **em veuen** *they see me*, **et veuen** *they see you*.

Indirect object pronouns

Latin	míhi/ me	tíbi/ te	ílli/ illíus	ílli/ illíus	nos	vos	íllis/ illórum	íllis/ illárum	síbi/ se
Portuguese	me	te	lhe	lhe	nos	vos	lhes	lhes	se
Galician	me	che	lle	lle	nos	vos	lles	lles	se
Spanish	me	te	le	le	nos	os	les	les	se
Catalan	me	te	li	li	nos	vos	lis	lis	se
Occitan	me	te	li	li	nos	vos	lor	lor	se
French	me	te	lui	lui	nous	vous	leur	leur	se
Romansh	ma	ta	al	la	ans	as	als	las	sa
Sardinian	mi	ti	li	li	nos	vos	lis	lis	si
Italian	mi	ti	gli	gli	ci	vi	loro	loro	si
Romanian	îmi	îţi	îi	îi	ne	vă	le	le	îşi
	to me	*to you*	*to him*	*to her*	*to us*	*to all of you*	*to them*	*to them (all fem.)*	*to him/herself, to themselves*

- All languages. General remarks about <u>direct object pronouns</u> also apply to this set of *indirect objects*. The forms of indirect object and direct object pronouns tend to overlap considerably. In most languages, only the third-person forms differ between direct and indirect object pronouns: French **tu me vois** *you see me* and **tu me dis** *you say to me* versus **tu le vois** *you see him* and **tu lui dis** *you say to him*.

- All languages. When a <u>verb</u> can take both indirect and direct object pronouns (<u>ditransitive</u>), the pronouns are placed in a strict order. The order is typically (subject) + indirect object + direct object + verb: French **je te le dis**, Italian **(io) te lo dico**, Romansh **jau t'al di**, Romanian **(eu) ţi-l spun**, Sardinian **(deo) ti lu naro** *I say it to you*. The treatment of <u>pronoun syntax</u> is complex and varies between languages.

Present Indicative

First conjugation

Romanian	Italian	Sardinian	Romansh	French	Occitan	Catalan	Spanish	Galician	Portuguese
cânt	canto	canto	chant(el)	chante	canti	canto	canto	canto	canto
cânți	canti	cantas	chantas	chantes	cantas	cantes	cantas	cantas	cantas
cântă	canta	cantat	chanta	chante	canta	canta	canta	canta	canta
cântăm	cantiamo	cantamus	chantain	chantons	cantam	cantem	cantamos	cantamos	cantamos
cântați	cantate	cantades	chantais	chantez	cantatz	canteu	cantáis	cantades	cantais
cântă	cantano	cantant	chantan	chantent	cantan	canten	cantan	cantan	cantam

Latin					
cánto	cántas	cántat	cantámus	cantátis	cántant
I sing	*you sing*	*(s)he sings*	*we sing*	*you all sing*	*they sing*

Notes on first <u>conjugation</u> verbs in the *present indicative* active:

- Romansh. Some verbs have a suffix **-el** in the first-<u>person</u> singular: **jau engraziel** (**engraziar**) *I thank* (*to thank*). Its use varies between dialects: Surselvan **jeu spereschel** vs. standard **jau speresch** *I hope*. Its use can also depend on the shape of the <u>stem</u>: **jau cumprel** (**cumprar**) *I buy* (*to buy*).

- Romansh. Some verbs add an augment **-esch-** between stem and suffix: **el sperescha** (**sperar**) *he hopes* (*to hope*). The **-esch-** disappears in the first and second-person plural: **nus sperain** *we hope*.

- Romanian. Some verbs add an augment **-ez-** between stem and suffix: **completezi** (**completa**) *you complete* (*to complete*). The third-person singular and plural suffix with augment is **-ează**: **(ei) completează** *they complete*. The **-ez-** disappears in the first and second-person plural: **completați** *all of you complete*.

- Romanian. The stem **cânt-** becomes **cânț-** before the second-person singular ending **-i**. This expected change is an example of Romanian *palatalization* before **-i**: **includ** *I include*, **includem** *we include* but **incluzi** and not ***includi** for *you include*.

PRESENT INDICATIVE

Second conjugation

Romanian	Italian	Sardinian	Romansh	French	Occitan	Catalan	Spanish	Galician	Portuguese
cad	temo		tem(el)				temo	temo	temo
cazi	temi		temas				temes	temes	temes
cade	teme		tema				teme	teme	teme
cădem	temiamo		temain				tememos	tememos	tememos
cădeți	temete		temais				teméis	temedes	temeis
cad	temono		teman				temen	temen	temem

Latin						
tímeo	tímes	tímet	timémus	timétis	tíment
I fear	*you fear*	*(s)he fears*	*we fear*	*you all fear*	*they fear*

Notes on second <u>conjugation</u> verbs in the *present indicative* active:

- Portuguese, Galician, Spanish. Many Latin second conjugation verbs show irregularities. Latin third conjugation verbs are also moved into this class: Vulgar Latin ***vívere** *to live* becomes Portuguese **viver**.

- Catalan, French, Occitan. These languages only retain a small set of *irregular verbs* in this conjugation. The <u>infinitive</u> ends in stressed **-er** in Catalan and Occitan: **voler** means *to want* in both languages. The Latin <u>infinitive</u> **-ére** becomes French **-oir** (pronounced /waʀ/): **vouloir** *to want*. Some ending-stressed **-ére** verbs become stem-stressed third conjugation verbs in these languages: Vulgar Latin ***debére** becomes Catalan and Occitan **deure** *to have to*.

- Sardinian. Latin **-ére** verbs are reassigned to the third (stem-stressed) conjugation: Sardinian **tìmere** *to fear* has the forms **timo, times, timet, timimus, timides, timen**.

- Romansh. Verbs from the second and third conjugations are distinguished by their infinitive: Latin **-ére** becomes Romansh **-air**, while unstressed **-ere** becomes **-er**.

- Romanian. Verbs in this conjugation have an infinitive in **-ea** and irregular forms: **pot, putem** (**putea**) *I can, we can* (*to be able*). The example verb is **a cădea** *to fall* instead of **a teme** *to fear* because Romanian **teme** is a regular **-e** (third conjugation) verb, not an **-ea** verb.

Third conjugation

Romanian	Italian	Sardinian	Romansh	French	Occitan	Catalan	Spanish	Galician	Portuguese
pierd	perdo	perdo	perd(el)	perds	pèrdi	perdo			
pierzi	perdi	perdes	perdas	perds	pèrdes	perds			
pierde	perde	perde	perda	perd	pèrde	perd			
pierdem	perdiamo	perdimus	perdain	perdons	perdèm	perdem			
pierdeți	perdete	perdides	perdais	perdez	perdètz	perdeu			
pierd	perdono	perdent	perdan	perdent	pèrdon	perden			

Latin					
pérdo	**pérdis**	**pérdit**	**pérdimus**	**pérditis**	**pérdunt**
I lose	*you lose*	*(s)he loses*	*we lose*	*you all lose*	*they lose*

Notes on third <u>conjugation</u> verbs in the *present indicative* active:

- Portuguese, Galician, Spanish. Western and Central Iberian languages redistribute third conjugation verbs into the second (stressed **-er**) or fourth (stressed **-ir**). Vulgar Latin ***dícere** *to say* (stressed on the <u>stem</u>) becomes Old Spanish **dezir** and Portuguese **dizer** (both stressed on the ending). Similarly, ***pérdere** *to lose* becomes Spanish and Portuguese **perder**. The result is a simple three-way distinction: **a** (**-ar** verbs), **e** (**-er** verbs), **i** (**-ir** verbs). Other Iberian languages like Asturian share this reduced system.

- Occitan. The verb stem alternates between stressed **pèrd-** and unstressed **perd-**.

- Romanian. The verb stem has changed from Latin **perd-** to Romanian **pierd-**.

PRESENT INDICATIVE

Fourth conjugation

Romanian	Italian	Sardinian	Romansh	French	Occitan	Catalan	Spanish	Galician	Portuguese
definesc	definisco	defino	definesch	définis	definissi	defineixo	defino	defino	defino
definești	definisci	definis	defineschas	définis	definisses	defineixes	defines	defines	defines
definește	definisce	definit	definescha	définit	definís	defineixe	define	define	define
definim	definiamo	definimus	definin	définissons	definissèm	definim	definimos	definimos	definimos
definiți	definite	definides	definis	définissez	definissètz	definiu	definís	definides	definis
definesc	definiscono	definint	defineschan	définissent	definisson	defineixen	definen	definen	definem

Latin					
definio	definis	definit	definimus	definítis	definint
I define	*you define*	*(s)he defines*	*we define*	*you all define*	*they define*

Notes on fourth <u>conjugation</u> verbs in the *present indicative* active:

- Catalan. Many verbs in this conjugation add an augment **-eix-** when the <u>stem</u> would be stressed. The augment is dropped in the first and second-<u>person</u> plural. The verb **preferir** *to prefer* has forms like **prefereixo, prefereixes, preferim** *I prefer, you prefer, we prefer*. Some verbs do not take the augment: **durmo, dormim** (**dormir**) *I sleep, we sleep* (*to sleep*).

- Occitan. Many verbs in this conjugation take the augment **-iss-** in all persons and numbers. The verb **preferir** *to prefer* has forms like **preferisses** *you prefer*. Some verbs do not take the augment: **venes, venèm** (**venir**) *you come, we come* (*to come*).

- French. Regular verbs take the augment **-is(s)-** in all persons and numbers. Some verbs, including **partir** *to leave*, are instead conjugated like third conjugation verbs: **je pars, tu pars, il part, nous partons, vous partez, ils partent**.

- Romansh. Many verbs take the augment **-esch-**, but the augment is dropped in the first and second plural. Some verbs, including **partir** *to leave*, are conjugated more like third conjugation verbs: **jau part, ti partas, el parta, nus partin, vus partis, els partan**.

- Italian. Many verbs take the augment **-isc-**, but the augment is dropped in the first and second-person plural. Verbs like **dormire** *to sleep* are conjugated more like third conjugation verbs: **dormo, dormi, dorme, dormiamo, dormite, dormono**.

- Romanian. Many verbs take the augment **-esc/-eşt-**, but the augment is dropped in the first and second plural. Some verbs, including **a dormi** *to sleep*, are conjugated more like third conjugation verbs: **dorm, dormi, doarme, dormim, dormiţi, dorm**.

PAST INDICATIVE (PRETERIT)

First conjugation

Romanian	Italian	Sardinian	Romansh	French	Occitan	Catalan	Spanish	Galician	Portuguese
cântai	cantai	cantei		chantai	cantèri	cantí	canté	cantei	cantei
cântaşi	cantasti	cantesti		chantas	cantères	cantares	cantaste	cantache	cantaste
cântă	cantò	canteit		chanta	cantèt	cantà	cantó	cantou	cantou
cântarăm	cantammo	cantemus		chantâmes	cantèrem	cantàrem	cantamos	cantamos	cantámos
cântaţi	cantaste	cantezis		chantâtes	cantèretz	cantàreu	cantasteis	cantastes	cantastes
cântă	cantarono	canterunt		chantèrent	cantèron	cantaren	cantaron	cantaron	cantaram

Latin	cantávi	cantavísti	cantávit	cantávimus	cantavístis	cantavérunt
	I sang	*you sang*	*(s)he sang*	*we sang*	*you all sang*	*they sang*

Notes on first <u>conjugation</u> verbs in the *past indicative* active:

- Catalan. Some dialects restrict this **passat simple** *simple past* to writing and prefer the **passat perifràstic** *periphrastic past* in conversation, which is built from **anar** *to go* + infinitive: **vaig cantar** *I sang* (standard) versus **cantí** *I sang* (literary).

- French. The use of this simple past is restricted to literature. The past tense is normally expressed with the **passé composé** *compound past*—**avoir** (Latin **habere** > ***abere**) + past participle of <u>transitive verbs</u> or **être** (Latin **esse** > ***essere**) + past participle of <u>intransitive</u> and <u>reflexive verbs</u>: **j'ai chanté** *I sang* (literally *I have sung*), **je suis parti** *I left* (literally *I am departed*).

- Romansh. Speakers replace the archaic past forms with **avair** *to have* plus the past participle of transitive verbs and **esser** *to be* plus the past participle of intransitive and reflexive verbs: **jau hai chantà** *I sang* (literally *I have sung*), **jau sun partì** *I left* (literally *I am departed*).

- Sardinian. Speakers use **àere** *to have* plus the past participle of transitive verbs or **èssere** *to be* plus the past participle of intransitive and reflexive verbs to refer to the past: **appo cantadu** *I sang*, **so partidu** *I left*.

- Italian. Many speakers limit this **passato remoto** *remote past* to literature and use the **passato prossimo** *near past* in conversation. The conversational past uses **avere** *to have* with the past participle of transitive verbs: **ho cantato** *I sang*. The verb **essere** *to be* is used with the past participle of intransitive and reflexive verbs: **sono partito** *I left*.

- Romanian. Speakers normally form the past with **avea** *to have* plus the past participle: **ai cântat** *you sang*. Aromanian speakers prefer past endings instead: Aromanian **cãntai** *I sang* (informal) versus Romanian **cântai** *I sang* (literary or dialectal).

Past Indicative (Preterit)

Second conjugation

Romanian	Italian	Sardinian	Romansh	French	Occitan	Catalan	Spanish	Galician	Portuguese
căzui	temei						temí	temín	temi
căzuși	temesti						temiste	temiche	temeste
căzu	temè/temette						temió	temeu	temeu
căzurăm	tememmo						temimos	tememos	tememos
căzurăți	temeste						temisteis	temestes	temestes
căzură	temerono/temettero						temieron	temeron	temeram

Latin	timui	timuísti	timuit	timúimus	timuístis	timuérunt
	I feared	*you feared*	*(s)he feared*	*we feared*	*you all feared*	*they feared*

Notes on second <u>conjugation</u> verbs in the *past indicative* active:

- Catalan, Occitan, French. These languages have a small number of <u>irregular verbs</u> that originate in this conjugation.
- Romanian. The Romanian verb **teme** *to fear* belongs to the third (<u>stem</u>-stressed) conjugation, so the example verb is **cădea** *to fall*.

PAST INDICATIVE (PRETERIT)

Third conjugation

Romanian	Italian	Sardinian	Romansh	French	Occitan	Catalan	Spanish	Galician	Portuguese
pierdui	persi	perdei		perdis	perdèri	perdí			
pierduși	perdesti	perdesti		perdis	perdères	perderes			
pierdu	perse	perdeit		perdit	perdèt	perdé			
pierdurăm	perdemmo	perdemus		perdîmes	perdèrem	perdérem			
pierdurăți	perdeste	perdezis		perdîtes	perdèretz	perdéreu			
pierdură	persero	perderunt		perdèrent	perdèron	perderen			

Latin	pérdidi	perdidísti	pérdidit	perdídimus	perdidístis	perdíderint
	I lost	*you lost*	*(s)he lost*	*we lost*	*you all lost*	*they lost*

Notes on third <u>conjugation</u> verbs in the *past indicative* active:

- Portuguese, Galician, Spanish. Iberian languages have moved these verbs into the second (**-ére**) and fourth (**-íre**) conjugations: Portuguese **perdi, perdeste, perdeu (perder)** *I lost, you lost, she/he lost (to lose)*.

Past Indicative (Preterit)

Fourth conjugation

Latin	(English)	Romanian	Italian	Sardinian	Romansh	French	Occitan	Catalan	Spanish	Galician	Portuguese
definívi	I defined	definii	definii	definei	definii	définis	definiguèri	definí	definí	definín	defini
definívisti	you defined	definiși	definisti	definesti	definisti	définis	definiguères	definires	definiste	definiche	definiste
definívit	(s)he defined	defini	definì	defineit		définit	definiguèt	definí	definió	definiu	definiu
definívimus	we defined	definirăm	definimmo	definemus		définîmes	definiguèrem	definírem	definimos	definimos	definimos
definívistis	you all defined	definirați	definiste	definezis		définîtes	definiguèretz	definíreu	definisteis	definistes	definistes
definivérunt	they defined	definiră	definirono	definerunt		définirent	definiguèron	definiren	definieron	definiron	definiram

Notes on fourth <u>conjugation</u> verbs in the *past indicative* active:

- All languages. General remarks about first conjugation verbs in the past tense still apply.

- Occitan. Regular **-ir** verbs add an augment **-igu-** before the signature past tense endings in **-èr-**: **definiguères** *you defined* and not **definères**. This applies both to **-ir** verbs that take a stem augment **-is(s)-** in the present indicative and those that do not.

IMPERFECT INDICATIVE

First conjugation

Romanian	Italian	Sardinian	Romansh	French	Occitan	Catalan	Spanish	Galician	Portuguese
cântam	cantavo	cantaio	chantava	chantais	cantavi	cantava	cantaba	cantaba	cantava
cântai	cantavi	cantaias	chantavas	chantais	cantavas	cantaves	cantabas	cantabas	cantavas
cânta	cantava	cantaiat	chantava	chantait	cantava	cantava	cantaba	cantaba	cantava
cântam	cantavamo	cantaiamus	chantavan	chantions	cantàvem	cantàvem	cantábamos	cantabamos	cantávamos
cântați	cantavate	cantaiazis	chantavas	chantiez	cantàvetz	cantàveu	cantábais	cantabades	cantáveis
cântau	cantavano	cantaiant	chantavan	chantaient	cantavan	cantaven	cantaban	cantaban	cantavam

Latin	cantábam	cantábas	cantábat	cantabámus	cantabátis	cantábant
	I used to sing	you used to sing	(s)he used to sing	we used to sing	you all used to sing	they used to sing

Notes on first <u>conjugation</u> verbs in the *imperfect indicative* active:

- All languages. The principal difference between the imperfect and the preterit (simple <u>past</u>) is the <u>aspect</u> of the verb—perfective (preterit) versus imperfective (imperfect). Unlike the preterit, the imperfect displays few <u>irregularities</u> across languages.

IMPERFECT INDICATIVE

Second conjugation

Romanian	Italian	Sardinian	Romansh	French	Occitan	Catalan	Spanish	Galician	Portuguese
căzeam	temevo		temeva				temía	temía	temia
cădeai	temevi		temevas				temías	temías	temias
cădea	temeva		temeva				temía	temía	temia
cădeam	temevamo		temevan				temíamos	temiamos	temíamos
cădeați	temevate		temevas				temíais	temiades	temíeis
cădeau	temevano		temevan				temían	temían	temiam

Latin					
timébam	timébas	timébat	timebámus	timebátis	timébant
I used to fear	*you used to fear*	*(s)he used to fear*	*we used to fear*	*you all used to fear*	*they used to fear*

Notes on second <u>conjugation</u> verbs in the *imperfect indicative* active:

- Catalan, Occitan, French, Sardinian. These languages have limited the second conjugation (ending-stressed **-ére**) in favor of the third (<u>stem</u>-stressed **-ere**). For example, French <u>infinitives</u> in **-oir** historically belong to this conjugation: **pouvoir** *to be able* has the imperfact forms **je pouvais, tu pouvais, il pouvait, nous pouvions, vous pouviez, ils pouvaient.**

IMPERFECT INDICATIVE

Third conjugation

Romanian	Italian	Sardinian	Romansh	French	Occitan	Catalan	Spanish	Galician	Portuguese
pierdeam	perdevo	perdio	perdeva	perdais	perdiái	perdia			
pierdeai	perdevi	perdias	perdevas	perdais	perdiás	perdies			
pierdea	perdeva	perdiat	perdeva	perdait	perdiá	perdia			
pierdeam	perdevamo	perdiamus	perdevan	perdions	perdiam	perdíem			
pierdeați	perdevate	perdiazis	perdevas	perdiez	perdiatz	perdíeu			
pierdeau	perdevano	perdian	perdevan	perdaient	perdián	perdien			

Latin	perdébam	perdébas	perdébat	perdebámus	perdebátis	perdébant
	I used to lose	you used to lose	(s)he used to lose	we used to lose	you all used to lose	they used to lose

Notes on third <u>conjugation</u> verbs in the *imperfect indicative* active:

- Galician, Spanish, Portuguese. Westen and Central Iberian languages redistribute verbs from this conjugation into the second and fourth conjugations. For example, ***vívere** *to live* becomes Spanish **vivir—vivía, vivías, vivía, vivíamos, vivíais, vivían.**

IMPERFECT INDICATIVE

Fourth conjugation

Romanian	Italian	Sardinian	Romansh	French	Occitan	Catalan	Spanish	Galician	Portuguese
definea	definivo	definio	definiva	définissais	definissiái	definia	definía	definía	definia
defineai	definivi	definias	definivas	définissais	definissiás	definies	definías	definías	definias
definea	definiva	definiat	definiva	définissait	definissiá	definia	definía	definía	definia
defineam	definivamo	definiamus	definivan	définissions	definissiam	definíem	definíamos	definíamos	definíamos
defineați	definivate	definiazis	definivas	définissiez	definissiatz	definíeu	definíais	definistes	definíeis
defineau	definivano	definiant	definivan	définissaient	definissián	definien	definían	definían	definiam

Latin	definibam	definibas	definibat	definibámus	definibátis	definibant
	I used to define	you used to define	(s)he used to define	we used to define	you all used to define	they used to define

Notes on fourth conjugation verbs in the _imperfect indicative_ active:

- Occitan, French. Verbs in this conjugation with a present tense augment **-iss-** retain that augment in the imperfect indicative: French **ils finissent, ils finissaient** (**finir**) _they finish, they used to finish (to finish)._

FUTURE INDICATIVE

First conjugation

Romanian	Italian	Sardinian	Romansh	French	Occitan	Catalan	Spanish	Galician	Portuguese
	canterò			chanterai	cantarai	cantaré	cantaré	cantarei	cantarei
	canterai			chanteras	cantaràs	cantaràs	cantarás	cantarás	cantarás
	canterà			chantera	cantarà	cantarà	cantará	cantará	cantará
	canteremo			chanterons	cantarem	cantarem	cantaremos	cantaremos	cantaremos
	canterete			chanterez	cantaretz	cantareu	cantaréis	cantaredes	cantareis
	canteranno			chanteront	cantaràn	cantaran	cantarán	cantarán	cantarão

Latin	*cantáre hábeo	*cantáre hábes	*cantáre hábet	*cantáre habémus	*cantáre habétis	*cantáre hábent
	I will sing	you will sing	(s)he will sing	we will sing	you all will sing	they will sing

Notes on first <u>conjugation</u> verbs in the *<u>future indicative</u>* active:

- Latin. Verbs had future indicative endings in Classical Latin: **amabo**, **amabis**, **amabimus** (**amare**) *I will love, you will love, we will love* (*to love*). In Western Romance, a new future was built by placing <u>present indicative</u> forms of Vulgar Latin ***abere** *to have* after the relevant <u>infinitive</u>.

- Portuguese, Galician, Spanish, Catalan, Occitan, French, Italian. This distinctive Western Romance construction is formed from Latin infinitive + ***abere** *to have*, which fused to form the future endings.

- Romansh. The future is expressed with **vegnir a** + infinitive: **jau vegn a chantar** *I will sing*.

- Sardinian. Speakers use constructions like **àere a** + infinitive to express the future: **tue as a cantare** *you will sing*.

- Romanian. Speakers use other constructions, including **o să** + present <u>subjunctive</u>, to express the future: **o să cânte** *they will sing*.

FUTURE INDICATIVE

Second conjugation

	Romanian	Italian	Sardinian	Romansh	French	Occitan	Catalan	Spanish	Galician	Portuguese
		temerò						temeré	temerei	temerei
		temerai						temerás	temerás	temerás
		temerà						temerá	temerá	temerá
		temeremo						temeremos	temeremos	temeremos
		temerete						temeréis	temeredes	temereis
		temeranno						temerán	temerán	temerão

Latin					
*timére hábeo	*timére hábes	*timére hábet	*timére habémus	*timére habétis	*timére hábent
I will fear	you will fear	(s)he will fear	we will fear	you all will fear	they will fear

Notes on second <u>conjugation</u> verbs in the *future indicative* active:

- Catalan, Occitan, French. The set of second conjugation verbs is limited and <u>irregular</u>: French **pouvoir** *to be able* has irregular future forms like **je pourrai**, **tu pourras**, **nous pourrons** *I will be able, you will be able, we will be able*. The third conjugation is favored: Vulgar Latin ending-stressed ***timére** *to fear* becomes Catalan <u>stem</u>-stressed **témer**.

FUTURE INDICATIVE

Third conjugation

Romanian	Italian	Sardinian	Romansh	French	Occitan	Catalan	Spanish	Galician	Portuguese
	perderò			perdrai	perdrai	perdré			
	perderai			perdras	perdràs	perdràs			
	perderà			perdra	perdrà	perdrà			
	perderemo			perdrons	perdrem	perdrem			
	perderete			perdrez	perdretz	perdreu			
	perderanno			perdront	perdràn	perdran			

Latin						
*pérdere hábeo	*pérdere hábes	*pérdere hábet	*pérdere habémus	*pérdere habétis	*pérdere hábent
I will lose	you will lose	(s)he will lose	we will lose	you all will lose	they will lose

Notes on third <u>conjugation</u> verbs in the *future indicative* active:

- Portuguese, Galician, Spanish. Iberian languages redistribute Latin third conjugation verbs into the second and fourth conjugations: Vulgar Latin <u>stem</u>-stressed ***pérdere** *to lose* becomes Galician ending-stressed **perder**.

Future Indicative

Fourth conjugation

	Romanian	Italian	Sardinian	Romansh	French	Occitan	Catalan	Spanish	Galician	Portuguese
		definirò			définirai	definirai	definiré	definiré	definirei	definirei
		definirai			définiras	definiràs	definiràs	definirás	definirás	definirás
		definirà			définira	definirà	definirà	definirá	definirá	definirá
		definiremo			définirons	definirem	definirem	definiremos	definiremos	definiremos
		definirete			définirez	definiretz	definireu	definiréis	definiredes	definireis
		definiranno			définiront	definiràn	definiran	definirán	definirán	definirão

Latin						
	*definíre hábeo	*definíre hábes	*definíre hábet	*definíre habémus	*definíre habétis	*definíre hábent
	I will define	*you will define*	*(s)he will define*	*we will define*	*you all will define*	*they will define*

Grammar Tables | 165

Notes on fourth <u>conjugation</u> verbs in the *future indicative* active:

- All languages. General remarks about first conjugation verbs in the future indicative still apply.

PRESENT SUBJUNCTIVE

First conjugation

	Romanian	Italian	Sardinian	Romansh	French	Occitan	Catalan	Spanish	Galician	Portuguese
	cânt	canti	cante	chantia	chante	cante	canti	cante	cante	cante
	cânţi	canti	cantes	chantias	chantes	cantes	cantis	cantes	cantes	cantes
	cânte	canti	cantet	chantia	chante	cante	canti	cante	cante	cante
	cântăm	cantiamo	cantemus	chantian	chantions	cantem	cantem	cantemos	cantemos	cantemos
	cântaţi	cantiate	cantezis	chantias	chantiez	cantetz	canteu	cantéis	cantedes	canteis
	cânte	cantino	cantent	chantian	chantent	canten	cantin	canten	canten	cantem

Latin	cántem	cántes	cántet	cantémus	cantétis	cántent
	[that] I sing	[that] you sing	[that] (s)he sing	[that] we sing	[that] you all sing	[that] they sing

Notes on first <u>conjugation</u> verbs in the *present subjunctive* active:

- Romansh. Verbs that take an augment **-esch-** between stem and suffix in the <u>present indicative</u> retain it in the present subjunctive: **ch'ella spereschia** (**sperar**) *that she hope* (*to hope*). The **-esch-** still disappears in the first and second-person plural: **che nus sperian** *that we hope*.

- Romanian. Verbs that add an augment **-ez-** between stem and suffix in the present indicative retain it in the present subjunctive: **să completeze** (**completa**) *that (s)he/they complete* (*to complete*). The augment **-ez-** still disappears in first and second-person plural: **să completăm** *that we complete*.

Second conjugation

Romanian	Italian	Sardinian	Romansh	French	Occitan	Catalan	Spanish	Galician	Portuguese
cad	tema		temia				tema	tema	tema
cazi	tema		temias				temas	temas	temas
cadă	tema		temia				tema	tema	tema
cădem	temiamo		temian				temamos	temamos	temamos
cădeți	temiate		temias				temáis	temades	temais
cadă	temano		temian				teman	teman	teman

Latin	tímeam	tímeas	tímeat	timeámus	timeátis	tímeant
	[that] I fear	[that] you fear	[that] (s)he fear	[that] we fear	[that] you all fear	[that] they fear

Notes on second <u>conjugation</u> verbs in the *present subjunctive* active:

- Portuguese, Galician, Spanish. Many Latin second conjugation verbs show <u>irregularities</u>. Latin third conjugation verbs are also moved into this class: ***vívere** *to live* becomes Portuguese **viver**— **viva**, **vivas**, **viva**, **vivamos**, **vivais**, **vivam**.

- Catalan, French, Occitan. These languages retain a small set of irregular verbs in this conjugation.

- Sardinian. Latin **-ére** verbs are reassigned to the third (<u>stem</u>-stressed) conjugation: Sardinian **tìmere** *to fear* has forms like **chi timas** *that you fear* and **chi timamus** *that we fear*.

- Romanian. Verbs in this conjugation have an infinitive in **-ea** and irregular forms: **să pot**, **să poată**, **să putem** (**putea**) *that I can, that he can, that we can (to be able)*. The example verb is **a cădea** *to fall* instead of **a teme** *to fear* because Romanian **teme** is a regular **-e** (third conjugation) verb, not an **-ea** verb: **să tem**, **să temi**, **să teamă**, **să temem**, **să temeți**, **să teamă**.

Third conjugation

Romanian	Italian	Sardinian	Romansh	French	Occitan	Catalan	Spanish	Galician	Portuguese
pierd	perda	perda	perd(el)	perde	pèrda	perdi			
pierzi	perda	perdes	perdas	perdes	pèrdas	perdis			
piardă	perda	perde	perda	perde	pèrda	perdi			
pierdem	perdiamo	perdamus	perdian	perdions	perdam	perdem			
pierdeți	perdiate	perdazis	perdias	perdiez	perdatz	perdeu			
piardă	perdano	perdant	perdian	perdent	pèrdan	perdin			

Latin	pérdam	pérdas	pérdat	perdámus	perdátis	pérdant
	[that] I lose	[that] you lose	[that] (s)he lose	[that] we lose	[that] you all lose	[that] they lose

Notes on third <u>conjugation</u> verbs in the *present subjunctive* active:

- Portuguese, Galician, Spanish. Iberian languages redistribute third conjugation verbs into the second conjugation (stressed **-er**) or the fourth conjugation (stressed **-ir**): Vulgar Latin ***dícere** *to say* becomes Portuguese **dizer** but Spanish **decir**. Similarly, Vulgar Latin ***pérdere** *to lose* changes into Portuguese and Spanish **perder**.

- Occitan. The verb <u>stem</u> alternates between stressed **pèrd-** and unstressed **perd-**.

- Romanian. The verb stem has changed from Latin **perd-** to Romanian **pierd-**.

PRESENT SUBJUNCTIVE

Fourth conjugation

Romanian	Italian	Sardinian	Romansh	French	Occitan	Catalan	Spanish	Galician	Portuguese
definesc	definisca	defina	defineschia	définisse	definisca	defineixi	defina	defina	defina
definești	definisca	definas	defineschias	définisse	definiscas	defineixis	definas	definas	definas
definească	definisca	definat	defineschia	définisse	definisca	defineixi	defina	defina	defina
definim	definiamo	definamus	definian	définissions	definiscam	definim	definamos	definamos	definamos
definiți	definiate	definazis	definias	définissiez	definiscatz	definiu	defináis	definades	definais
definească	definiscano	definant	defineschian	définissent	definiscan	defineixin	definan	definan	definam

Latin					
definiam	**definias**	**definiat**	**definiámus**	**definiátis**	**definiant**
[that] I define	[that] you define	[that] (s)he define	[that] we define	[that] you all define	[that] they define

Notes on fourth <u>conjugation</u> verbs in the *present subjunctive* active:

- Catalan. Verbs in this conjugation that take an augment **-eix-** in the <u>present indicative</u> retain it in the present subjunctive: **preferir** *to prefer* has the subjunctive forms **prefereixi, prefereixis, prefereixi, preferim, preferiu, prefereixin**. Notice that the augment is still dropped in the first and second person plural. Some verbs do not take the augment: **dormir** *to sleep* has the forms **dormi, dormis, dormi, dormim, dormiu, dormin**.

- Occitan. Verbs in this conjugation that take an augment **-iss-** in the present indicative have **-isc-** in the present subjunctive: **preferir** *to prefer* has the subjunctive forms **preferisca, preferiscas, preferiscam, preferiscam, preferiscatz, preferiscan**.

- French. Regular verbs take the augment **-iss-** in all persons and numbers. Some verbs, including **partir** *to leave*, are instead conjugated like third conjugation verbs: **que je parte, que tu partes, qu'il parte, que nous partions, que vous partez, qu'ils partent**.

- Romansh. Verbs in this conjugation that take an augment **-eix-** in the present indicative retain it in the present subjunctive. The augment is dropped in the first and second plural. Some verbs, including **partir** *to leave*, are conjugated like third conjugation verbs: **che jau partia, che ti partias, ch'el partia, che nus partian, che vus partias, ch'els partian**.

- Italian. Verbs that take an augment **-isc-** in the present indicative retain it in the present subjunctive. The augment is dropped in the first and second plural. Some verbs, like **dormire** *to sleep*, are conjugated more like third conjugation verbs: **dorma, dorma, dorma, dormiamo, dormiate, dormano**.

- Romanian. Verbs with an augment **-esc-/-eşt-** in the present indicative retain it in the subjunctive. The augment is dropped in the first and second plural. Some verbs, including **a dormi** *to sleep*, resemble third conjugation verbs: **dorm, dormi, să doarmă, dormim, dormiți, să doarmă**.

IMPERFECT SUBJUNCTIVE

First conjugation

Romanian	Italian	Sardinian	Romansh	French	Occitan	Catalan	Spanish	Galician	Portuguese
	cantassi	cantàrepo	chantass	chantasse	cantèsse	cantés	cantase	cantase	cantasse
	cantassi	cantares	chantassas	chantasses	cantèsses	cantessis	cantases	cantases	cantasses
	cantasse	cantaret	chantass	chantât	cantèsse	cantés	cantase	cantase	cantasse
	cantassimo	cantàremus	chantassan	chantassions	cantèssem	cantéssim	cantásemos	cantasemos	cantássemos
	cantaste	cantàrezis	chantassas	chantassiez	cantèssetz	cantéssiu	cantaseis	cantasedes	cantásseis
	cantassero	cantarent	chantassan	chantassent	cantèsson	cantessin	cantasen	cantasen	cantassem

Latin	cantássem	cantásses	cantásset	cantassémus	cantassétis	cantássent
	[if] I sang	[if] you sang	[if] (s)he sang	[if] we sang	[if] you all sang	[if] they sang

Notes on first <u>conjugation</u> verbs in the *imperfect subjunctive* active:

- Latin. The forms given here are actually in the <u>pluperfect</u> subjunctive, which becomes the imperfect subjunctive in most of Romance. The original Latin imperfect subjunctive contained endings with **-re-**: **cantarem**, **cantares** and so on.

- French. The imperfect subjunctive is replaced by the <u>imperfect indicative</u> in common use: **si elle chantait** *if she sang*.

- Spanish. The imperfect subjunctive listed here derives from the Latin <u>pluperfect</u> subjunctive, giving forms with **-se-**: **si cantase**, **si cantases**, **si cantásemos** *if I sang, if you sang, if we sang*. Spanish speakers have another set of imperfect subjunctive forms from the Latin pluperfect indicative, which gives endings with **-ra-**: **si cantara**, **si cantaras**, **si cantáramos** *if I sang, if you sang, if we sang*. The two forms may vary freely in most situations.

- Sardinian. The Latin imperfect subjunctive endings survive in Sardinian, where speakers have endings with **-re-** instead of the originally <u>pluperfect</u> **-sse-**.

- Romanian. Speakers use the construction **să fi** + past participle to express the past subjunctive: **să fi cântat** *I should have sung*.

IMPERFECT SUBJUNCTIVE

Second conjugation

Romanian	Italian	Sardinian	Romansh	French	Occitan	Catalan	Spanish	Galician	Portuguese
	temessi		temess				temiese	temese	temesse
	temessi		temessas				temieses	temeses	temesses
	temesse		temess				temiese	temese	temesse
	temessimo		temessan				temiésemos	temesemos	temêssemos
	temeste		temessas				temieseis	temesedes	temêsseis
	temessero		temessan				temiesen	temesen	temessem

Latin	timéssem	timésses	timésset	timessémus	timessétis	timéssent
	[if] I feared	[if] you feared	[if] (s)he feared	[if] we feared	[if] you all feared	[if] they feared

Notes on second <u>conjugation</u> verbs in the *imperfect subjunctive* active:

- Catalan, Occitan, French, Sardinian. These languages have limited the second conjugation (ending-stressed **-ére**) in favor of the third (<u>stem</u>-stressed **-ere**).

IMPERFECT SUBJUNCTIVE

Third conjugation

Romanian	Italian	Sardinian	Romansh	French	Occitan	Catalan	Spanish	Galician	Portuguese
	perdessi	perdèrepo	perdess	perdisse	perdèsse	perdés			
	perdessi	pèrderes	perdessas	perdisses	perdèsses	perdessis			
	perdesse	pèrderet	perdess	perdit	perdèsse	perdés			
	perdessimo	perderemus	perdevan	perdissions	perdèssem	perdéssim			
	perdeste	perderezis	perdessas	perdissiez	perdèssetz	perdéssiu			
	perdessero	pèrderent	perdessan	perdissent	perdèsson	perdessin			

Latin					
pérdissem	**pérdisses**	**pérdisset**	**perdissémus**	**perdissétis**	**pérdissent**
[if] I lost	*[if] you lost*	*[if] (s)he lost*	*[if] we lost*	*[if] you all lost*	*[if] they lost*

Notes on third <u>conjugation</u> verbs in the *imperfect subjunctive* active:

- Galician, Spanish, Portuguese. Western and Central Iberian languages redistribute verbs from this conjugation into the second and fourth conjugations.

Fourth conjugation

Romanian	Italian	Sardinian	Romansh	French	Occitan	Catalan	Spanish	Galician	Portuguese
	definisse	definirepo	definiss	définisse	definiguèsse	definís	definiese	definise	definisse
	definissi	definires	definissas	définisses	definiguèsses	definisses	definieses	definises	definisses
	definisse	definiret	definiss	définit	definiguèsse	definís	definiese	definise	definisse
	definissimo	definiremus	definissan	définissions	definiguèssem	definíssim	definiésemos	definisemos	definíssemos
	definiste	definirezis	definissas	définissiez	definiguèssetz	definíssiu	definieseis	definisedes	definísseis
	definissero	definirent	definissan	définissent	definiguèsson	definissin	definiesen	definisen	definissem

Latin	
definissem	[if] I defined
definisses	[if] you defined
definisset	[if] (s)he defined
definissémus	[if] we defined
definissétis	[if] you all defined
definíssent	[if] they defined

Notes on fourth <u>conjugation</u> verbs in the *imperfect subjunctive* active:

- All languages. General remarks about first conjugation verbs in the imperfect subjunctive still apply.

IMPERATIVE

First conjugation

Romanian	Italian	Sardinian	Romansh	French	Occitan	Catalan	Spanish	Galician	Portuguese
cântă	**canta**	**canta**	**chanta**	**chante**	**canta**	**canta**	**canta**	**canta**	**canta**
cântaţi	**cantate**	**cantate**	**chantai**	**chantez**	**cantatz**	**canteu**	**cantad**	**cantade**	**cantai**

Latin	
cánta	**cantáte**
sing!	*(all of you) sing!*

Notes on first <u>conjugation</u> verbs in the *imperative mood*:

- All languages. The table above gives direct singular and plural commands: Latin **cánta** *(you) speak!* versus **cantáte** *(all of you) sing!* Speakers may also state a wish or a command for any person and number using the <u>present subjunctive</u>: Spanish **¡que canten!** *let them sing!*, Romanian **să cânte!** *let them sing!* The first-person plural has an isolated optative or command form taken from the present subjunctive: Iberian **cantemos!**, Italian **cantiamo!** mean *let's sing!*

- All languages. The formation of the *negative imperative* varies. Some languages, including French and Rhaeto-Romansh, simply use the imperative with a negative particle: Romansh **chanta betg!**, **chantai betg!** *do not sing!, do not all of you sing!* Iberian languages (including Catalan) employ the present subjunctive with the negative particle: Spanish **¡no cantes!** *do not sing!* Italian and Romanian use an <u>infinitive</u> in the singular: Italian **non cantare!**, **non cantate!** *do not sing!, do not (all of you) sing!*

- Portuguese, Galician, Spanish, Catalan. Third-person subjunctive forms are used in polite or formal commands: Portuguese **cante!** *sing! (formal)*. Modern Portuguese and Latin American Spanish use third person forms for all plural commands, formal or informal: Portuguese **cantem!**, Spanish **¡canten!** *(all of you) sing!*

- Romansh. Verbs that take an augment **-esch-** between the <u>stem</u> and suffix in the <u>present indicative</u> retain it in the imperative: **sperescha!** *hope!* The **-esch-** still disappears in the plural.

- Romanian. Verbs that add an augment **-ez-** between stem and suffix in the present indicative retain it in the imperative: **completează!** *complete!* The **-ez-** still disappears in the plural.

IMPERATIVE

Second conjugation

	Romanian	Italian	Sardinian	Romansh	French	Occitan	Catalan	Spanish	Galician	Portuguese
	cazi	**teme**		**teme**				**teme**	**teme**	**teme**
	cădeți	**temete**		**temei**				**temed**	**temede**	**temei**

Latin		
time	**timéte**
fear!	*(all of you) fear!*

Notes on second <u>conjugation</u> verbs in the *<u>imperative mood</u>*:

- Catalan, French, Occitan, Sardinian. These languages (except Sarinian) retain only a small set of <u>irregular verbs</u> in this conjugation. All favor the third conjugation: Vulgar Latin ending-stressed ***timére** *to fear* becomes Catalan <u>stem</u>-stressed **témer** and Sardinian stem-stressed **tìmere**.

- Romanian. Verbs in this conjugation have an <u>infinitive</u> in **-ea** and irregular forms. The example verb is **a cădea** *to fall* instead of **a teme** *to fear* because Romanian **teme** is a regular **-e** (third conjugation) verb, not an **-ea** verb.

IMPERATIVE

Third conjugation

Romanian	Italian	Sardinian	Romansh	French	Occitan	Catalan	Spanish	Galician	Portuguese
pierde	perde	perde	perda	perd	pèrd	perd			
pierdeți	perdete	perdite	perdai	perdez	perdètz	perdeu			

Latin	
pérde	pérdite
lose!	(all of you) lose!

Notes on third <u>conjugation</u> verbs in the *<u>imperative mood</u>*:

- Portuguese, Galician, Spanish. Iberian languages redistribute third conjugation verbs into the second conjugation (stressed **-er**) or the fourth conjugation (stressed **-ir**): Vulgar Latin ***dícere*** *to say* becomes Spanish **decir** but Portuguese **dizer**, while ***pérdere*** *to lose* changes into Portuguese and Spanish **perder**, which is a second conjugation verb.

Fourth conjugation

Romanian	Italian	Sardinian	Romansh	French	Occitan	Catalan	Spanish	Galician	Portuguese
definește	**definisce**	**defini**	**definischa**	**définis**	**definís**	**defineix**	**define**	**define**	**define**
definiți	**definite**	**definite**	**defini**	**définissez**	**definissètz**	**definiu**	**definid**	**definide**	**defini**

Latin		
defini	*define!*	
definite		*(all of you)* *define!*

Notes on fourth <u>conjugation</u> verbs in the *imperative mood*:

- Catalan. Verbs that take the augment **-eix-** in the <u>present indicative</u> retain it in the imperative. Notice that the augment is still dropped in the second-person plural. Some verbs do not take the augment: **dorm!, dormiu!** (**dormir**) *sleep!, [all of you] sleep!* (*to sleep*).

- Occitan. Verbs that take the augment **-iss-** in the present indicative have **-ís** and **-issètz** in the imperative.

- French. Regular verbs still take the augment **-is(s)-**. Some verbs have unaugmented forms, such as **partir** *to leave*: **pars!, partez!**

- Romansh. Verbs that take an augment **-esch-** in the present indicative retain it in the imperative. The augment is dropped in the plural. Some verbs, like **partir** *to leave*, remain unaugmented: **parta!, parti!**

- Italian. Verbs that take an augment **-isc-** in the present indicative retain it in the imperative. The augment is dropped in the plural. Some verbs, such as **dormire** *to sleep*, do not take the augment: **dorme!, dormite!**

- Romanian. Verb with an augment **-esc/-eşt-** in the present indicative retain it in the imperative. The augment is dropped in the plural. Some verbs, including **a dormi** *to sleep*, remain unaugmented: **doarme!, dormiţi!**

CONDITIONAL

First conjugation

Romanian	Italian	Sardinian	Romansh	French	Occitan	Catalan	Spanish	Galician	Portuguese
	canterei			chanterais	cantariái	cantaria	cantaría	cantaría	cantaria
	canteresti			chanterais	cantariás	cantaries	cantarías	cantarías	cantarias
	canterebbe			chanterait	cantariá	cantaria	cantaría	cantaría	cantaria
	canteremmo			chanterions	cantariam	cantaríem	cantaríamos	cantariamos	cantaríamos
	cantereste			chanteriez	cantariatz	cantarieu	cantaríais	cantariades	cantaríeis
	canterebbero			chanteraient	cantarián	cantarien	cantarían	cantarían	cantariam

Latin		
*cantáre habébam/ hábui	*cantáre habébas/ habuísti	*cantáre habébat/ hábuit
I would sing	you would sing	(s)he would sing
*cantáre habebámus/ habuímus	*cantáre habebátis/ habuístis	*cantáre habébant/ habuérunt
we would sing	you all would sing	they would sing

Notes on first <u>conjugation</u> verbs in the *<u>conditional</u>*:

- Portuguese, Galician, Spanish, Catalan, Occitan, French, Italian. This distinctive Western Romance construction is formed from the Vulgar Latin infinitive plus <u>imperfect indicative</u> forms of ***abere** *to have*, which fused to form the conditional endings.

- Romansh. The conditional is expressed with the <u>imperfect subjunctive</u>: **jau chantass** *I would sing*.

- Sardinian. Speakers use constructions like the imperfect of **dèvere** *ought* (Latin **debére**) + <u>infinitive</u> for the present conditional: **tue dias cantare** *you would sing*.

- Italian. The conditional is built with the <u>perfect</u> of Vulgar Latin ***abere** rather than the imperfect, which French and Iberian use: ***finire abuerunt** gives **finirebbero** *they would finish*.

- Romanian. Speakers construct the conditional with a <u>helping verb</u> plus the infinitive: **aş cânta, am cânta, ar cânta** *I would sing, we would sing, they would sing*.

CONDITIONAL

Second conjugation

Romanian	Italian	Sardinian	Romansh	French	Occitan	Catalan	Spanish	Galician	Portuguese
	temerei						temería	temería	temeria
	temeresti						temerías	temerías	temerias
	temerebbe						temería	temería	temeria
	temeremmo						temeríamos	temeríamos	temeríamos
	temereste						temeríais	temeriades	temeríeis
	temerebbero						temerían	temerían	temeriam

Latin					
*timére habébam/ hábui	*timére habébas/ habuísti	*timére habébat/ hábuit	*timére habebámus/ habuímus	*timére habebátis/ habuístis	*timére habébant/ habuérunt
I would fear	*you would fear*	*(s)he would fear*	*we would fear*	*you all would fear*	*they would fear*

Notes on second <u>conjugation</u> verbs in the *<u>conditional</u>*:

- All languages. General remarks about the first conjugation still apply.
- Catalan, Occitan, French. The set of second conjugation verbs is limited and <u>irregular</u>. The third conjugation is favored: Latin ending-stressed **timére** *to fear* becomes Catalan <u>stem</u>-stressed **témer**.

CONDITIONAL

Third conjugation

Romanian	Italian	Sardinian	Romansh	French	Occitan	Catalan	Spanish	Galician	Portuguese
	perderei			perdrais	perdriái	perdria			
	perderesti			perdrais	perdriás	perdries			
	perderebbe			perdrait	perdriá	perdria			
	perderemmo			perdrions	perdriam	perdríem			
	perdereste			perdriez	perdriatz	perdríeu			
	perderebbero			perdraient	perdrián	perdrien			

Latin					
*pérdere habébam/ hábui	*pérdere habébas/ habuísti	*pérdere habébat/ hábuit	*pérdere habebámus/ habuímus	*pérdere habebátis/ habuístis	*pérdere habébant/ habuérunt
I would lose	*you would lose*	*(s)he would lose*	*we would lose*	*you all would lose*	*they would lose*

Notes on third <u>conjugation</u> verbs in the *conditional*:

- All languages. General remarks about the first conjugation still apply.
- Portuguese, Galician, Spanish. Iberian languages redistribute Latin third conjugation verbs into the second and fourth conjugations: Latin <u>stem</u>-stressed **pérdere** *to lose* becomes Galician ending-stressed **perder**.

Conditional

Fourth conjugation

Romanian	Italian	Sardinian	Romansh	French	Occitan	Catalan	Spanish	Galician	Portuguese
	definírei			définirais	definiríái	definiria	definiría	definiría	definiria
	definiresti			définirais	definiriás	definiries	definirías	definirías	definirias
	definirebbe			définirait	definiriá	definiria	definiría	definiría	definiria
	definiremmo			définirions	definiriam	definiríem	definiríamos	definiriamos	definiríamos
	definireste			définiriez	definiriatz	definiríeu	definiríais	definiriades	definiríeis
	definirebbero			définiraient	definirían	definirien	definirían	definirían	definiriam

Latin						
*definíre habébam/ hábui	*definíre habébas/ habuísti	*definíre habébat/ hábuit	*definíre habebámus/ habuímus	*definíre habebátis/ habuístis	*definíre habébant/ habuérunt
I would define	*you would define*	*(s)he would define*	*we would define*	*you all would define*	*they would define*

Notes on fourth <u>conjugation</u> verbs in the *<u>conditional</u>*:

- All languages. General remarks about the first conjugation still apply. It's worth repeating that Iberian and French languages rely on <u>imperfect</u> forms of ***abere** *to have* to build the conditional, while Italian opts for <u>preterit</u> forms of ***abere**: Western Romance ***definire abebas** *you used to have to define* becomes Occitan **definiriás** *you would define* but ***definire abuisti** *you had to define* gives Italian **definiresti** *you would define*.

NON-FINITE FORMS

First conjugation

	infinitive	gerund	present participle	past participle
Latin	cantáre	cantándum	cantántem	cantátum
Portuguese	cantar	cantando		cantado
Galician	cantar	cantando		cantado
Spanish	cantar	cantando		cantado
Catalan	cantar	cantant	cantant	cantat
Occitan	cantar	cantant	cantant	cantat
French	chanter	chantant	chantant	chanté
Romansh	chantar	chantond		chantà
Sardinian	cantare	cantande		cantadu
Italian	cantare	cantando	cantante	cantato
Romanian	cânta	cântând		cântat
	to sing	*singing*	*singing*	*sung*

- All languages. The *participles* allow speakers to form <u>adjectives</u> out of verbs. Present participles relate to ongoing actions and past participles to completed ones: Italian **la donna cantante** *the singing woman*, **l'inno cantato** *the sung hymn*.

- All languages. The Latin <u>present participle</u> is limited in most modern languages. They have a set of adjectives and <u>nouns</u> formed with the participle, but do not treat these words as grammatical verb forms: Spanish **cantante** *singer* is not necessarily treated like a form of **cantar** *to sing*. On the other hand, the <u>past participle</u> is widely used, including in <u>perfect</u> and <u>passive</u> constructions.

- Catalan, Occitan, French. The <u>gerund</u> and present participle have the same form: Latin **cantantem** becomes French **chantant**, while Latin **cantandum** also turns into French **chantant**.

NON-FINITE FORMS

Second conjugation

	infinitive	gerund	present participle	past participle
Latin	**timére**	**timéndum**	**timéntem**	***tímitum**
Portuguese	**temer**	**temendo**		**temido**
Galician	**temer**	**temendo**		**temido**
Spanish	**temer**	**temiendo**		**temido**
Catalan				
Occitan				
French				
Romansh	**temair**	**temend**		**temì**
Sardinian				
Italian	**temere**	**temendo**	**temente**	**temuto**
Romanian	**cadea**	**căzând**		**căzut**
	to fear	*fearing*	*fearing*	*feared*

- Latin. The Vulgar Latin past participle was shifted to ***timítu** or ***timútu**: Spanish **temido**, Italian **temuto** *feared*.

- Catalan, French, Occitan, Sardinian. Apart from Sardinian, these languages retain a small set of <u>irregular verbs</u> in this <u>conjugation</u>. All favor the third conjugation: Latin ending-stressed **timére** becomes Catalan <u>stem</u>-stressed **témer** and Sardinian stem-stressed **tìmere**.

- Romanian. Verbs in this conjugation have an infinitive in **-ea** and irregular forms. The example verb is **a cădea** *to fall* instead of **a teme** because Romanian **teme** is a regular **-e** (third conjugation) verb, not an **-ea** verb.

Non-Finite Forms

Third conjugation

	infinitive	gerund	present participle	past participle
Latin	pérdere	perdéndum	perdéntem	pérditum
Portuguese				
Galician				
Spanish				
Catalan	perdre	perdent	perdent	perdut
Occitan	pèrdre	perdent	perdent	perdut
French	perdre	perdant	perdant	perdu
Romansh	perder	perdend		perdì
Sardinian	pèrdere	perdende		pérdidu
Italian	perdere	perdendo	perdente	perduto
Romanian	pierde	pierzând		pierdut
	to lose	*losing*	*losing*	*lost*

- Latin. The Vulgar Latin past participle was shifted to ***perdítu** or ***perdútu**: Spanish **perdido**, Italian **perduto** *lost*.

- Portuguese, Galician, Spanish. Iberian languages redistribute third conjugation verbs into the second conjugation (stressed **-er**) or the fourth conjugation (stressed **-ir**).

Fourth conjugation

	infinitive	gerund	present participle	past participle
Latin	**definíre**	**definiéndum**	**definiéntem**	**definítum**
Portuguese	definir	definindo		definido
Galician	definir	definindo		definido
Spanish	definir	definiendo		definido
Catalan	definir	definint	definint	definit
Occitan	definir	definissent	definissent	definit
French	définir	définissant	définissant	défini
Romansh	definir	definind		definì
Sardinian	definire	defininde		definidu
Italian	definire	definendo	definente	definito
Romanian	defini	definind		definit
	to define	*defining*	*defining*	*defined*

▪ Occitan, French. Verbs with an augment **-is(s)-** in the <u>present indicative</u> retain it in the <u>gerund</u>. Compare augmented **finissant** (**finir**) *finishing* (*to finish*) to unaugmented **partant** (**partir**) *leaving* (*to leave*).

PHRASES & SENTENCES

Noun phrases with an adjective before the noun

Vulgar Latin	*illa/issa forma correcta
Portuguese	a forma correta
Galician	a forma correcta
Spanish	la forma correcta
Catalan	la forma correcta
Occitan	la forma condrecha
French	la forme correcte
Romansh	la furma correcta
Sardinian	sa forma zusta
Italian	la forma corretta
Romanian	forma corectă
	the correct form

- All languages. Romance <u>adjectives</u> tend to follow the <u>nouns</u> they modify. The "regular" or unmarked Romance pattern places adjectives to the right of the <u>article</u> and noun—determiner + noun + adjective: Italian **un'idea importante** *an important idea,* **l'idea importante** *the important idea.*

- Romanian. Like all Romanian nouns, the feminine noun **formă** *form* attaches the definite article as a suffix: Vulgar Latin ***forma illa** becomes **forma** *the form.*

Noun phrases with an adjective after the noun

Vulgar Latin	*illa/issa nova lingua
Portuguese	a nova língua
Galician	a nova lingua
Spanish	la nueva lengua
Catalan	la nova llengua
Occitan	la nòva lenga
French	la nouvelle langue
Romansh	la nova lingua
Sardinian	sa nova limba
Italian	la nuova lingua
Romanian	noua limbă
	the new language

- All languages. Few Romance <u>adjectives</u> regularly precede the modified <u>noun</u>. With a few frequently used adjectives, the adjective's position determines its meaning: French **une certaine idée** *a certain idea* but **une idée certaine** *a sure idea*, Portuguese **as grandes línguas** *the great tongues* versus **as línguas grandes** *the big tongues*.

- All languages. A small but frequently used set of metaphorical "qualities" (like *good, bad, great* or *beautiful*) regularly precedes the noun: Portuguese **boa ideia** *good idea*.

- All languages. Most adjectives fall to the right, but speakers can sometimes construct a marked or less literal <u>phrase</u> by moving adjectives from the right to the left of the noun: Spanish **una correcta idea** is marked, and is less frequent than unmarked **una idea correcta** *a correct idea*.

- Romanian. When an adjective precedes a noun, the <u>definite article</u> attaches to the adjective instead of the noun: **o nouă limbă** *a new language*, **noua limbă** *the new language*.

Noun phrases with possessives & determiners

Vulgar Latin	*illa/issa mea lingua materna
Portuguese	(a) minha língua materna
Galician	a miña lingua materna
Spanish	mi lengua materna
Catalan	la meva llengua materna
Occitan	la meuna lenga mairenala
French	ma langue maternelle
Romansh	mia lingua materna
Sardinian	sa mea limba materna
Italian	la mia lingua materna
Romanian	limba mea maternă
	my native language

- All languages. Some Romance languages (like Romanian, Italian and Sardinian) use <u>possessives</u> with a <u>definite article</u>, while others (like French, Spanish and Romansh) only have the possessive: Romanian **limba mea** (literally *language-the my*) versus French **ma langue** (literally *my language*). Many languages, including Spanish and Italian (but not French), also allow an <u>indefinite article</u> and a possessive: Portuguese **uma boa ideia minha** *a good idea of mine*.

- All languages. <u>Demonstratives</u>, <u>interrogatives</u>, <u>negatives</u> and other Romance <u>determiners</u> act like the possessives in languages like Spanish and French. In other words, even languages with article+possessive+noun drop the article when they use these determiners: Sardinian **custas limbas** *these languages* but not *sas custas limbas.

- Catalan, Occitan. Like <u>adjectives</u>, possessives in these languages occur with a definite article. Both languages also have a shorter "weak" set of possessives, which replace the definite article: Catalan **el meu pare** or **mon pare** for *my father*.

- Portuguese. Possessives occur both with and without the definite article: **minha história** or **a minha história** for *my history*.

Sentences with comparative adjectives

Vulgar Latin	*Illu/issu linguaticu est mais/plus importante qua/de illa/issa technica.
Portuguese	A linguagem é mais importante (do) que a técnica.
Galician	A linguaxe é máis importante que a técnica.
Spanish	El lenguaje es más importante que la técnica.
Catalan	El llenguatge és més important que la tècnica.
Occitan	Lo lengatge es mai important que la tecnica.
French	Le langage est plus important que la technique.
Romansh	Il linguatg è pli impurtant che la tecnica.
Sardinian	Su limbazu est prus importante de sa tennica.
Italian	Il linguaggio è più importante della tecnica.
Romanian	Limbajul este mai important decât tehnica.
	Language is more important than technique.

- All languages. Romance languages compare two <u>nouns</u> using a <u>comparative adjective</u> in a construction akin to English *more (adjective) than (noun)*. Languages differ in whether they inherit ***mais** (like Spanish) or ***plus** (like Italian) for *more*. They also differ in how they express *than*—some have **que/che** (like Romansh, French and Spanish), others **de** (like Italian and Sardinian).

- Italian, Sardinian. The comparative particle comes from Latin **de** *of*. The construction with **che** *that* is used before words other than nouns: Sardinian **prus mannu chi si potat imadzinare** *larger than can be imagined*, Italian **più importante che bello** *more important than beautiful*.

- Portuguese. This construction has a variant with and without the word **do**.

Basic affirmative sentences

Vulgar Latin	*(Tu) studias una nova lingua.
Portuguese	(Tu) estudas uma nova língua.
Galician	(Ti) estudas unha nova lingua.
Spanish	(Tú) estudias una nueva lengua.
Catalan	(Tu) estudies una nova llengua.
Occitan	(Tu) estúdias una nòva lenga.
French	Tu étudies une nouvelle langue.
Romansh	Ti studegias ina nova lingua.
Sardinian	(Tue) istudias una nova limba.
Italian	(Tu) studi una nuova lingua.
Romanian	(Tu) studiezi o nouă limbă.
	You study a new language.

- All languages. The <u>*basic word order*</u> for all these languages is <u>subject</u> (*you*) + <u>verb</u> (*study*) + <u>object</u> (*a new language*). This example contains an object <u>noun phrase</u> with the structure <u>indefinite article</u> + <u>adjective</u> + <u>noun</u> in all languages. The adjective precedes the modified noun because of the specific adjective chosen. Most Romance adjectives would appear to the right of the noun. Also, most Romance languages have more flexible word order than English. Sentences regularly depart from this basic word order: Spanish **¿es correcta la frase?** *is the phrase correct?* (literally *is correct the phrase?*).

- All languages. <u>Subject pronouns</u> are dropped in most of Romance (<u>pro-drop</u>): Spanish **hablas latín** *you speak Latin*. Their inclusion may indicate emphasis: Spanish **tú hablas latín** *YOU speak Latin*. French and Romansh are two clear exceptions.

- French, Romansh. Unlike Latin and most of modern Romance, these languages no longer drop their subject pronouns: French **je parle latin** but not ***parle latin** for *I speak Latin*.

Basic negative sentences

Vulgar Latin	*(Tu) non studias una nova lingua.
Portuguese	(Tu) não estudas uma nova língua.
Galician	(Ti) non estudas unha nova lingua.
Spanish	(Tú) no estudias una nueva lengua.
Catalan	(Tu) no estudies una nova llengua.
Occitan	(Tu) estúdias pas una nòva lenga.
French	Tu n'étudies pas une nouvelle langue.
Romansh	Ti na studegias betg ina nova lingua.
Sardinian	(Tue) no(n) istudias una nova limba.
Italian	(Tu) non studi una nuova lingua.
Romanian	(Tu) nu studiezi o nouă limbă.
	You don't study a new language.

- All languages. Most Romance languages use a reflex of Latin **non** or **ne** *not* before the <u>verb</u> in <u>negations</u>.

- Occitan, French. Negation is achieved by placing **pas** after the verb, which has come to mean *not* in these languages. Standard French also adds **ne** in front of the verb, which speakers tend to omit in everyday use: **j'parle pas** *I do not speak.* Occitan only uses **pas**: **ieu parli pas.** Catalan also has this same **pas**, which can optionally reinforce a negative: **(jo) no parlo pas** *I do NOT speak* versus **no parlo** *I don't speak.*

- Romansh. In basic negations, **na** comes before a verb and **betg** after. This resembles the French use of **ne...pas**.

Sentences with multiple negations

Vulgar Latin	*(Tu) non vides nunqua/(ia)mais nulla ren nata.
Portuguese	(Tu) nunca vês nada.
Galician	(Ti) nunca ves nada.
Spanish	(Tú) nunca ves nada.
Catalan	(Tu) no veus mai res.
Occitan	(Tu) veses pas jamai res.
French	Tu ne vois jamais rien.
Romansh	Ti na vesas mai nagut.
Sardinian	(Tue) non vides mai nudda.
Italian	(Tu) non vedi mai niente.
Romanian	(Tu) nu vezi niciodată nimic.
	You don't ever see anything.

- All languages. The sentence above actually has the Romance structure [you] *not see never nothing* (in Catalan, Romanian, Italian and other languages) or [you] *never see nothing* (in Spanish, Portuguese and Galician). The Romance languages welcome multiple negation (so-called "double negatives" and "triple negatives") in sentences. Languages retain the negative particle (usually Latin **non**) before the verb, drop negatives after the verb (like French **pas**) and accumulate negations to the right of the verb.

- Portuguese, Galician, Spanish. Iberian languages place some negations alongside Latin **non** but allow other negations to replace the **non**. The basic negative particle is present alongside **nada** in Portuguese **você não viu nada** *you saw nothing*, but makes no appearance with **nunca** in **você nunca viu** *you never saw (it)* (compare the word order to **você não viu nunca**). The verb also drops its negative particle when the subject is negative: **ninguém fala** *nobody speaks*. These Portuguese uses have parallels in the other Ibero-Romance languages.

- Catalan, Occitan, French, Romansh. Any post-verbal negative (like French **pas** or Romansh **betg**) is dropped and negations are added to the right of the verb: French **il ne voit pas** *he doesn't see* versus **il ne voit jamais rien** *he never sees anything*. The same structure applies when the negative is the subject, except here the negative comes before the verb: French **personne ne voit rien** *nobody sees anything* and **personne ne parle** *nobody speaks*, Catalan **ningú no sap** *nobody knows*.

- Italian, Sardinian, Romaninan. The Central and Eastern Romance languages leave **non** in place and add further negations to the right of the verb. The Romanian verb's negative particle still stays in place when the negative is a subject: **nimeni nu poate** *nobody can* (literally *nobody not can*). On the other hand, Sardinian and Italian may act like the Iberian languages when it comes to negative subjects: Sardinian **neune potet**, Italian **nessuno può** both mean *nobody can*.

Questions with question words (who, what, etc.)

Vulgar Latin	*Quid voles/queris (tu)?
Portuguese	(O) que queres (tu)?
Galician	Que queres (ti)?
Spanish	¿Qué quieres (tú)?
Catalan	Què vols (tu)?
Occitan	Què vòles (tu)?
French	Qu'est-ce que tu veux ?
Romansh	Tge vuls ti?
Sardinian	Ite cheres (tue)?
Italian	Che vuoi (tu)?
Romanian	Ce vrei (tu)?
	What do you want?

- All languages. The <u>question word</u> is normally brought to the front (left) of the question, and the languages may "invert" word order by moving the <u>subject</u> to the right of the verb (if the subject is not the question word): Romanian **ce ştie el?** *what does he know?*

- All languages. Most languages routinely drop subject pronouns (<u>pro-drop</u>). The basic structure of these example questions leaves out the personal pronoun: Sardinian **ite cheres?**, Spanish **¿qué quieres?** and so on. French and Romansh are the exceptions.

- Portuguese, Galician. The interrogative **o que?** *what?* has a variant with and without **o**. A construction using the circumlocution **é que** *is [it] that* between the interrogative and main sentence is also found: Portuguese **o que é que queres?** *what is it that you want?*

- French. In the standard language, speakers insert **est-ce que** *is it that* between the interrogative word and the basic sentence: **quand est-ce que tu pars ?** *When do you leave?* The formal language also sees "inversion" of the subject and verb: **quand pars-tu ?** *when do you leave?* Colloquial French enjoys the possibility of even more straightforward word orders: **quand tu pars?** or **tu pars quand?** for *when do you leave?*

Questions without question words (yes-no)

Vulgar Latin	*Studias (tu) una nova lingua?
Portuguese	Estudas (tu) uma nova língua?
Galician	Estudas (ti) unha nova lingua.
Spanish	¿Estudias (tú) una nueva lengua?
Catalan	Estudies (tu) una nova llengua?
Occitan	Estúdias (tu) una nòva lenga?
French	Est-ce que tu étudies une nouvelle langue?
Romansh	Estudegias ti una nova lingua?
Sardinian	(A) istudias (tue) una nova limba?
Italian	Studi (tu) una nuova lingua?
Romanian	(Tu) studiezi o nouă limbă?
	Are you studying a new language?

- All languages. <u>*Yes-no questions*</u> may <u>move</u> the <u>subject</u> to the right of the <u>verb</u>. When possible (as in Latin, Portuguese and Italian), languages that can <u>pro-drop</u> subject pronouns do so: Catalan **parles llatí?** *do you speak Latin?*, Romanian **ştie?** *does she know?*

- All languages. Questions are often asked with the <u>basic word order</u> and a change in intonation, especially in conversation: French **tu parles latin ?**, Italian **tu parli latino?** *do you speak Latin?* The position of dropped subject pronouns remains hidden: Italian **parli latino?** *[do you] speak Latin?* In Romanian, subject-verb is the default order for yes-no questions: **tu ştii?** *do you know?*

- French. In the standard language, speakers insert **est-ce que** *is it that* before the subject and verb, which preserves the word order of the main clause: **est-ce que tu pars ?** *are you leaving?* The formal language also permits inversion of the subject and verb, which moves the subject to the right of the verb (as in other Romance languages): **pars-tu ?** *are you leaving?* Colloquial French can maintain the declarative word order: **tu pars?** *are you leaving?*

- Sardinian. The particle **a** may begin a yes-no question. The subject then drops or moves to the right of the verb: **a ses tue?** *are you?*

Sentences with an indicative dependent clause

Vulgar Latin	*(Ille/Isse) confirmat quod illa/issa forma non est correcta.
Portuguese	(Ele) confirma que a forma não é correta.
Galician	(El) confirma que a forma non é correcta.
Spanish	(Él) confirma que la forma no es correcta.
Catalan	(Ell) confirma que la forma no és correcta.
Occitan	(El) conferma que la forma es pas condrecha.
French	Il confirme que la forme n'est pas correcte.
Romansh	El conferma che la furma n'è betg correcta.
Sardinian	(Isse) cunfirmat chi sa forma non est zusta.
Italian	(Lui) conferma che la forma non è corretta.
Romanian	(El) confirmă că forma nu este corectă.
	He confirms that the form is not correct.

- All languages. Refer to the tables and notes on basic sentence structure for information on the <u>word order</u> of <u>noun phrases</u>, <u>affirmative</u> and <u>negative</u> statements, and <u>questions</u>. General remarks about basic phrases and sentences still apply here.

- All languages. Languages with the <u>subject pronoun</u> in parentheses tend to drop the subject pronoun: Italian **confermò che sono giusti** *[he] confirmed that [they] are right*.

- All languages. Statements that involve a finite verb followed by an <u>infinitive</u> in English tend to have a *that* <u>clause</u> in Romance. This is particularly expected when the subjects of the two clauses differ: French **je sais qu'elle est honnête** (literally *I know that she is honest*) and not *je sais la être honnête** (*I know her be honest*) for *I know her to be honest*.

Sentences with a subjunctive dependent clause

Vulgar Latin	*(Nos) querimus/volemus quod Maria veniat.
Portuguese	(Nós) queremos que venha (a) Maria.
Galician	(Nós) queremos que veña Maria.
Spanish	(Nosotros) queremos que venga María.
Catalan	(Nosaltres) volem que Maria vingui.
Occitan	(Nosautres) volèm que Maria venga.
French	Nous voulons que Marie vienne.
Romansh	Nus vulain che Maria vegnia.
Sardinian	(Nois) cherimus chi benzat Maria.
Italian	(Noi) vogliamo che Maria vegna.
Romanian	(Noi) vrem să vină Maria.
	We want that Mary come / Mary to come.

- All languages. <u>Subject pronouns</u> are optional in most Romance languages: **confermò che sono giusti** *[he] confirmed that [they] are right*. The subject may fall to the right of the <u>verb</u> (verb before subject) in many languages: Galician **...que Maria veña** and **...que veña Maria** for *...that Maria come*. Romanian demands this order in the <u>subjunctive</u>: **să vină el** but not ***să el vină** for *that he come*.

- All languages. Statements that involve a finite verb followed by an <u>infinitive</u> in English tend to have a *that* <u>clause</u> in Romance, particularly when the subjects of the two clauses differ: Italian **voglio che siano** *I want them to be* (literally *[I] want that [they] are*). This is a noteworthy feature of subjunctive clauses, since the subjunctive is normally rendered as <u>object</u> + infinitive in English.

- French. Speakers commonly use the pronoun **on** with a third-person singular verb for *we*, especially in conversation: **on veut qu'elle vienne** *we want her to come*.

- Romanian. Uniquely, speakers join two finite verbs with the particle **să**, not **că** (cognate to Romance **que/che**). The verb after **să** takes the subjunctive: Romanian **vreau să vezi** *I want you to see* (literally *[I] want that [you] see*).

Sentences with a finite verb + infinitive in the main clause

Vulgar Latin	*(Nos) querimus/volemus studiare.
Portuguese	(Nós) queremos estudar.
Galician	(Nós) queremos estudar.
Spanish	(Nosotros) queremos estudiar.
Catalan	(Nosaltres) volem estudiar.
Occitan	(Nosautres) volèm estudiar.
French	Nous voulons étudier.
Romansh	Nus vulain studegiar.
Sardinian	(Nois) cherimus istudiare.
Italian	(Noi) vogliamo studiare.
Romanian	(Noi) vrem să studiem.
	We want to study.

- All languages. This Romance construction is mainly found when the <u>subject</u> of the <u>infinitive</u> is identical to the subject of the <u>main clause</u>: Spanish **nosotros queremos ganar** *we want (us) to win*. Romance does not structure these sentences as ***nos potemus quod nos videmus** *we can that we see*. Romanian presents a clear exception.

- All languages. Romance verbs of <u>perception</u> and sense may be followed by an infinitive with a different subject. The resulting structure parallels English and Latin <u>accusative + infinitive</u>: Spanish **yo la oigo cantar** *I hear her sing*, Italian **mi ha visto partire** *[he] saw me leave*.

- French. Speakers commonly use the pronoun **on** with a third-person singular verb for *we*, especially in conversation: **on veut venir** *we want to come*.

- Romanian. Uniquely, speakers join two finite verbs with the particle **să**. The verb that follows **să** takes the <u>subjunctive mood</u>: Romanian **vreau să văd** *I want to see* (literally *[I] want that [I] see*) and not ***vreau vedea** (literally *[I] want to see*).

Imperative sentences

Vulgar Latin	*Confirma quod est correctu!
Portuguese	Confirma que é correto!
Galician	Confirma que é correcto!
Spanish	¡Confirma que es correcto!
Catalan	Confirma que és correct!
Occitan	Conferma que es condrech!
French	Confirme que c'est correct!
Romansh	Conferma ch'igl è correct!
Sardinian	Cunfirma chi est zustu!
Italian	Conferma ch'è corretto!
Romanian	Confirmă că este corect!
	Confirm that it is correct!

- All languages. The second-person singular <u>command</u> forms are given. Languages have a corresponding plural, and many languages have different <u>polite</u> and <u>negative</u> forms, which are typically derived from the <u>subjunctive</u>: Spanish **confirma** *confirm (informal)*, **confirme / confirme usted** *confirm (formal)*, **no confirmes** *do not confirm (informal)*, and so on.

- French, Romansh. These languages require a <u>subject</u> in the <u>dependent clause</u>, so a generic third-person pronoun is added: French **ce** in **c'est correct** *it's correct*.

Reflexive sentences

Vulgar Latin	*(Ille/Isse) se presentat.
Portuguese	(Ele) se apresenta.
Galician	(El) se presenta.
Spanish	(Él) se presenta.
Catalan	(Ell) es presenta.
Occitan	(El) se perpara.
French	Il se présente.
Romansh	El sa preschenta.
Sardinian	(Isse) si presentat.
Italian	(Lui) si presenta.
Romanian	(El) se prezintă.
	He introduces himself.

- All languages. The word order of <u>subjects</u>, <u>*reflexive pronouns*</u> and <u>verbs</u> parallels each language's general treatment of subjects, <u>objects</u> and verbs: compare Italian **(lei) mi presenta** *she introduces me* to **(io) mi presento** *I introduce myself*. Specifically, object pronouns stick close to the left side of the main verb: French **je le lui dis** *I tell it to him* (literally *I it to-him say*).

- All languages. This reflexive structure is very common throughout Romance. Some verbs occur primarily with reflexive pronouns, and others have a different meaning when reflexive pronouns are attached: Spanish **yo voy** *I go* but **yo me voy** *I leave* (literally *I go myself*). You can review each language's use of direct and indirect reflexive pronouns in the tables of personal <u>object pronouns</u>.

- Iberian languages. Ibero-Romance may traditionally place object pronouns, including reflexives, after the verb. This tendency is strongest in Western Iberia, particularly in Portuguese: **Maria apresentou-se** *Mary introduced herself*. The tight connection between verb and object pronoun is put on display when formal Portuguese suffixes pronouns to <u>infinitives</u> in <u>future</u> and <u>conditional</u> constructions: Portuguese **eles apresentar-se-ão** (literally *they introduce-themselves-will*) versus Spanish **ellos se presentarán** (literally *they themselves introduce-will*) for *they will introduce themselves*.

- Italian. When the reflexive occurs alongside a third-person direct object, the reflexive falls to the right rather than the left of the direct object: **lo si pensa** instead of the expected *se lo pensa for *she thinks it to herself*.

- Romanian. Speakers have access to both a direct (<u>accusative</u>) reflexive pronoun **se** and a separate indirect (<u>dative</u>) reflexive pronoun **îşi**. Pronoun choice depends on the verb: **îşi aranjează părul** *[he] fixes [his] hair* (literally *he to-himself arranges the hair*) versus **se spală părul** *[he] washes [his] hair* (literally *he himself washes the hair*).

Sentences with multiple object pronouns

Vulgar Latin	*(Tu) mi illu/oc das.
Portuguese	(Tu) dás-mo.
Galician	(Ti) dasmo.
Spanish	(Tú) me lo das.
Catalan	(Tu) m'ho dónes.
Occitan	(Tu) me o dònas.
French	Tu me le donnes.
Romansh	Ti m'al das.
Sardinian	(Tue) mi lu das.
Italian	(Tu) me lo dai.
Romanian	(Tu) mi-l dai.
	You give it to me.

- All languages. The basic Romance <u>*direct*</u> and <u>*indirect object pronouns*</u> are affixed to or lean against the <u>verb</u>. Typically, the core construction consists of indirect object + direct object + verb, but the structure and usage varies from language to language.

- Spanish. An indirect third-person pronoun plus a direct third-person pronoun yields an unexpected outcome: **se lo digo** but not ***le lo digo** for *I say it to her/him*, and **se lo digo** but not ***les lo digo** for *I say it to them*.

- Portuguese. Vowel-final indirect object pronouns contract with the third-person direct objects **o, a, os, as**: **eu lho disse** *I said it to him*, which combines **lhe** *to him / to her* with **o** *it*.

- Portuguese, Galician. Pronouns may attach or fall to the right of the verb instead of the left: Portuguese **dei-lho** or **eu lho dei** for *I gave it to him/her*. The two uses are not identical.

- Portuguese, Latin. Third-person direct objects may be suppressed when understanding is assumed: Portuguese **dou-lhe** *I give [it] to her* instead of the full **dou-lho**.

- Aragonese, Catalan, Occitan, French, Sardinian, Italian. <u>Partitives</u> (for English *of it / from there / some*) and <u>locatives</u> (for English *to it / there*) exist in these languages right alongside the normal object pronouns: French **je t'en remercie** *I thank you for it* (literally *I you of it thank*). As above, these <u>clitics</u> fall to the right of any object pronouns. The partitive follows the locative: Sardinian **bi nd'est meta** *there's a lot of it* (literally *there of it is much*).

- Occitan. The order of pronouns varies depending on the dialect: **me o dònas** or **o me dònas** for *[you] give it to me.*

- Catalan, French, Romansh, Romanian. The full forms of pronouns with a final vowel contract with a following pronoun beginning in a vowel: Catalan **jo t'ho dic** *I tell it to you* contracts **te** + **ho** (*you* + *it*), and French **je m'y perds** *I lose myself in it / I get lost* contracts **me** + **y** (*me* + *there*).

- Catalan, Occitan, French, Romansh, Italian, Sardinian, Romanian. Object pronouns may contract before a verb begining with a vowel. Some languages apply this contraction as a rule (like French), others optionally (as Italian): Italian has **dicono che m'amano** alongside **dicono che mi amano** for *[they] say that [they] love me.*

- French. The order of indirect and direct pronouns shifts when two third-person pronouns are involved: **elle me le dit** and not *__*elle le me dit** for *she says it to me*, but **je le lui dis** and not *__*je lui le dis** for *I say it to her.*

- Spanish, Romanian. Speakers may reinforce the indirect object pronoun with full forms of <u>strong object pronouns</u>: Spanish **a mí no me lo da** and Romanian **nu mi-l da mie** for *he doesn't give it to me.*

Passive sentences

Vulgar Latin	*Totu se preparat.
Portuguese	Tudo prepara-se.
Galician	Todo se prepara.
Spanish	Todo se prepara.
Catalan	Tot es prepara.
Occitan	Tot s'alestís.
French	On prépare tout.
Romansh	Tot vegn preparà.
Sardinian	Totu si preparat.
Italian	Tutto si prepara.
Romanian	Totul se prepară.
	Everything is prepared.

- All languages. The <u>passive</u> is typically expressed with a third-person <u>reflexive</u> in Romance: Vulgar Latin ***illa cena se preparat ad sic** *the dinner is prepared this way* (literally *the dinner prepares itself this way*), Sardinian **si mandigat su casu** *the cheese is eaten* (literally *the cheese eats itself*). Notice the <u>word order</u> and <u>agreement</u>—subjects may follow the reflexive verb, and the reflexive verb agrees with the subject in most languages: Sardinian **si fraigat una cosa, si fraigan medas cosas** *one thing is made, many things are made.*

- All languages. The Romance <u>past participle</u> has a passive meaning when used as an <u>adjective</u>: Spanish **las comidas preparadas** *prepared meals.* Languages can express the corresponding active subject when necessary (as in English *prepared by someone*): Romanian **scris de un autor anonim** and Spanish **escrito por un autor anónimo** both translate to *written by an anonymous author.*

- All languages. Many languages allow full or "true" passives involving Latin ***essere** or ***stare** (*to be*) with a past participle and an optional agent (English *by someone/something*): Italian **la cena è preparata (da Maria)** *the dinner is prepared (by Mary).* This passive structure is common in writing but avoided in everyday speech:

Galician **é escrito polo autor** [it] *is written by the author* versus **o autor escribiuno** *the author wrote it*. The clear exception is Romansh.

- French. Speakers avoid the passive structures noted above by using the <u>pronoun</u> **on** (*one/we*, historically *man/person*) alongside an active verb: **on l'a fait** *it has been done* (literally *one it has done*). French still uses past participles plus an agent: **c'est écrit par quel écrivain ?** *it is written by which author?* Some sentences even endorse the pan-Romance use of reflexives for passives: **petit à petit, le problème se résout** *little by little, the problem is resolving itself / being resolved*.

- Catalan, Occitan. Speakers use both the reflexive and true passives. The reflexive object **se** flips to **es** before a consonant in Catalan: **es prepara** *is prepared* but **preparar-se** *to be prepared*. An equivalent to the French use of **on** also exists in literary language: Catalan **hom l'escriu**, Occitan **òm l'escriu** for *one writes it / it is written*. This structure is formal or archaic for Catalan and Occitan speakers, but the French parallel is common in conversation.

- Romansh. The standard language forms the passive with **vegnir** *to come* and a past participle: **construir ina chasa** *to build a house*, **ina chasa vegn construida** *a house is built* (literally *a house comes built*), **ina chasa è vegnì construida** *a house was built* (literally *a house is come built*).

Pronunciation of Romance

This section offers a rough sketch of the _pronunciation_ of Vulgar Latin, which subsequently divided into distinct Romance pronunciation systems. Remarks about the significant sound changes that differentiate the modern languages from Latin are included.

BASIC PRONUNCIATION OF COMMON ROMANCE

Letter	IPA pronunciation	English equivalent	Vulgar Latin example
a	/a/	aisle	*casa
e (ĕ / è)	/ɛ/	let	*bene
e (ē / é)	/e/	they	*potere
e (unstressed)	/ə/	about	(some of Romance)
i	/i/	thing	*si
i (before or after a vowel)	/j/	yearn	*iuvene
o (ŏ / ò)	/ɔ/	law (British)	*possu
o (ō / ó)	/o/	sow	*sole
u	/u/	rune	*tu
u (before or after a vowel)	/w/	wear	*suave
b, d, f, l, m, n, s, v, x		(as in English)	
p	/p/	space	*patre
t	/t/	stay	*tale
c + a/o/u	/k/	escape	*casa
c + e/i	/kj/ (Sardinian /k/)	cute	*celu
g + a/o/u	/g/	gate	*gustu
g + e/i	/gj/ (Sardinian /g/)	argue	*gente
h	(silent)	hour	*homine

Letter	IPA pronunciation	English equivalent	Vulgar Latin example
li + vowel	/lj/ or /ʎ/	million	*muliere
n + c/g	/ŋ/	ring	*lingua
gn	/ŋn/	sing now	*magnu
ni + vowel	/nj/ or /ɲ/	opinion	*balniu
qu	/kw/	squid	*quando
gu	/gw/	language	*lingua
r	/r/	(trilled)	*arte

VOWELS

Latin has five basic _vowels_, which explains the existence of five vowel letters in the Roman alphabet.

Basic Latin Vowels		
vowel	IPA	similar English sound
a	/a/	aisle
e	/e/	they
i	/i/	sing
o	/o/	tow
u	/u/	rue

- The letters **i** and **u** can also spell the consonants /j/ and /w/ before or after another vowel.

- Classical Latin has five long vowels corresponding to each of the five short vowels above—ā ē ī ō ū: Classical Latin **esse** /esse/ _to be_ versus **ēsse** /eːsse/ _to eat_. Such vowels are held longer than their short counterparts.

- Sardinian reduces the ten long and short vowels to just the five cardinal vowels. Many other Romance languages still maintain a difference between ē versus e and ō versus o. Romance languages apart from Sardinian also treat short i like long ē.

Latin & Romance Vowels				
Latin vowel	Classical	Western Romance	Sardinian	Romanian
a	/a/	/a/	/a/	/a/
ā	/a:/			
e	/e/	/ɛ/	/e/	/e/
ē	/e:/	/e/		
i	/i/		/i/	
ī	/i:/	/i/		/i/
o	/o/	/ɔ/	/o/	/o/
ō	/o:/	/o/		
u	/u/	/o/ or /u/	/u/	/u/
ū	/u:/	/u/		

Diphthongs

Latin speakers pronounced _diphthongs,_ including the very common **au** (pronounced /aw/) and **ae** (pronounced /ai/). As the centuries wore on, these diphthongs were shortened towards /e/ and /o/.

Latin & Romance Diphthongs				
Latin dipthong	Latin example	Portuguese example	Italian example	Sardinian example
ae	*quaestione	questão	questione	chestione
au	*paucu	pouco	poco	pagu

Diphthongs sometimes appear for Vulgar Latin /ɛ/ (short **e**) and /ɔ/ (short **o**) in <u>stressed</u> syllables.

Open Vowel > Romance Diphthong					
vowel	Latin example	Portuguese example	Spanish example	Italian example	French example
/ɛ/	*vɛnis	vens	vienes	vieni	viens
/ɔ/	*mɔrit	morre	muere	muore	meurt

Nasal vowels

French, Catalan, Portuguese and other languages have _nasal vowels_ before **n** or **m** and another consonant, or before **n** or **m** at the end of a word: Vulgar Latin ***manu** > ***man** becomes French **main** /mɛ̃/ and ***abante** turns into French **avant** /avɑ̃/.

The nasal may be dropped in some languages: earlier ***man** > Catalan **mà** /ma/. Portuguese and Campidanese have a history of intervocalic nasalization and nasal dropping: Vulgar Latin ***luna** becomes Old Portuguese **lũa** and then Modern Portuguese **lua**, while most languages have cognates like Italian **luna** or French **lune**.

CONSONANTS

At the beginning of words and after another consonant, Latin _consonants_ remain somewhat stable across Romance. The pronunciation table at the beginning of this chapter summarizes the pronunciation of consonants. Still, the Romance languages display variations worth mentioning even in this brief treatment of the pronunciation.

- The Latin consonant /h/ is lost in Romance: Classical Latin **hōra** /hoːra/ becomes Vulgar Latin ***ora**, Spanish /oɾa/, French /œʁ/, Romansh /ura/. Some languages keep the historical **h** in spelling: Spanish **hora** versus Romansh **ura**.

- Voiceless /s/ is voiced to /z/ between vowels in many languages, but not in Spanish or Romanian: Italian **casa** /kaza/ versus Romanian **casă** /kasə/.

- _Double consonants_ (geminates) are retained in Italy (where they are still held long) but appear as a single consonant elsewhere: Latin ***flamma** becomes Italian /fjamma/ but French /flam/, Spanish /jama/, Sardinian /frama/.

- _Consonant clusters_ are frequently altered, assimilated or simplified: Vulgar Latin ***factu** (with /kt/) but Italian **fatto**, Old Spanish **fecho** /fetʃo/, Galician **feito** and Romanian **fapt**. Initial clusters **pl** /pl/ and **cl** /kl/ provide clear examples of variation across the family:

Vulgar Latin *plovet > French pleut, Catalan plou versus Italian piove, Portuguese chove, Spanish llueve, Sardinian proet.

*Sign for the **piazza del Colosseo** ("plaza of the Colosseum") in Rome. The nouns **piazza** /pjattsa/ and **Colosseo** /kolosseo/ both contain geminate consonants.*

Palatalization

The palatal consonant /j/—a "y" sound written i or j in Latin—altered the pronunciation of consonants that it followed. Also, the vowels i and e came to alter the pronunciation of a preceding c /k/ or g /g/ outside of Sardinia. Lastly, the vowel a altered the way a preceding c or g was pronounced in Switzerland and France. All of these changes involve moving the tongue closer to the palate (roof of the mouth), a process called _palatalization_.

- The consonant /j/ tends to turn into an affricate or a fricative: *iustu /justu/ > Italian giusto /dʒusto/, Sardinian zustu /dzustu/, Romanian just /ʒust/, Spanish justo /xusto/.

- Consonants followed by /j/ get palatalized in all of Romance. The outcome of palatalized stops often contains /ts/ or /tʃ/ or their voiced counterparts (/dz/ and /dʒ/): Latin *gratia /gratja/ becomes Italian grazia /grattsia/ and *diurnu /djurnu/ gives Italian giorno

/dʒorno/. Western languages simplify these affricates to /s/, /z/, /ʃ/ and /ʒ/: *gratia also becomes Catalan gràcia /gɾasiə/ and *diurnu is the source of French jour /ʒuʁ/. Sometimes the /j/ that originally triggered the palatalization disappears: Portuguese graça /gɾasɐ/, French grâce /gʁas/.

- The sound of c and g turns palatal before e and i in almost all of Romance: Latin *facemus /fakemus/ becomes Portuguese fazemos /fazemus/, Old Spanish facemos /fatsemos/, Spanish hacemos /asemos/ and Romanian facem /fatʃem/. This parallels the pronunciation of c and g in English act versus ace and bag versus age. The clear exception is Sardinia, where /k/ and /g/ remain velar: Sardinian fachimus /fakimus/ or faghimus /fagimus/.

- The consonants c and g are palatalized to /tʃ/ (French /ʃ/) and /dʒ/ (French /ʒ/) before the vowel a in much of Swiss and French Romance: *caru becomes French cher /ʃɛʁ/, Romansh char /tɕar/ and *gamba becomes French jambe /ʒãb/.

Lenition

To the north and west of Central Italy, stop consonants are weakened between vowels—they become voiced stops in Portuguese, voiced fricatives in Spanish and are lost altogether in French. The next table demonstrates this weakening or _lenition_ of intervocalic consonants in Western Romance.

Romance Lenition					
	Vulgar Latin	Portuguese	Spanish	French	Italian
/p/	*supre/*supra	/sobri/	/soβre/	/syr/	/sopra/
/t/	*contatu	/kõtadu/	/kontaðo/	/kõte/	/kontato/
/k/	*aqua	/agwɐ/	/aɣwa/	/o/	/ak:wa/
	voiceless stop /p t k/	voiced stop /b d g/	voiced fricative /β ð ɣ/	deleted /Ø/	(not lenited) /p t k/

SYLLABLES

Basic Romance _syllables_ begin with a consonant or vowel and end in a vowel or a consonant—(C)V(C). Consonant clusters have CC or, infrequently, CCC(C): Sardinian **istimat** /is.ti.mat/, Catalan **blocs** /blɔks/, French **fenêtre** /fnɛtʁ/, Romanian **câți** /kɨts/. CV or CVC syllables are extremely common: Italian **pericolo** /pe.ri.ko.lo/, Spanish **ves** /bes/, Romanian **până** /pɨ.nə/, French **décidèrent** /de.si.dɛʁ/. The vowel nucleus may be filled by _diphthongs_ or _nasal vowels_: Occitan **pauc** /pawk/, Romanian **foarte** /fwar.te/, French **prendre** /pʁɑ̃dʁ/.

Accent

The second-to-last (penultimate) syllable or the third-to-last (antepenultimate) syllable of words carries a _stress accent_ in Latin: ***amare** /aˈma.re/ _to love_, ***populu** /ˈpo.pu.lu/ _people_. Syllable length originally determined stress placement in Latin—long penults were stressed. Single-syllable words are either stressed or, if they are _clitics_, unstressed: Vulgar Latin ***per oc** /per ˈo/ _however_ (stressed _pronoun_ ***oc** and unstressed _preposition_ ***per**).

Stress regularly falls on the penult when a word ends in a _vowel_ or one of the Western _plural_ endings (**n** and **s**): Italian **amare** /aˈmaː.re/, Spanish **decides** /deˈsi.ðes/, Catalan **decideixen** /də.siˈðɛ.ʃən/, Romansh **chasas** /ˈtɕa.zas/. Many languages also retain words stressed on the third-to-last syllable: Spanish **próspero** /ˈpɾos.pe.ɾo/, Italian **repubblica** /reˈpub.bli.ka/. However, the Romance languages of France force antepenultimate stress onto the penultimate syllable: Vulgar Latin ***prospera** /ˈprospera/ versus Occitan **prospèra** /pruˈspɛrɔ/.

Romance languages treat stressed vowels differently than unstressed ones, allowing a wider variety of vowels and dipthongs in stressed syllables. For example, Catalan has /a ɛ e i ɔ o u/ in stressed syllables but only /i ə u/ in unstressed syllables. French, Catalan, Occitan, Romansh and Romanian drop final unstressed vowels other than **-a**, which may weaken to /ə/ (as in Romanian and Catalan) or even disappear altogether (as in French).

*Rio de Janeiro with the **Pão de Açúcar** ("Sugarloaf [Mountain]") roughly centered. The Portuguese word **açúcar** has three syllables (/a.su.kaχ/) and is stressed on the penultimate syllable (/aˈsu.kaχ/).*

Elision

Romance languages preserve stressed syllables, while unstressed syllables are subject to <u>elision</u>. Languages see the loss of final unstressed vowels or even whole syllables at the end of a word: Vulgar Latin ***veritate** /veriˈtate/ becomes Sardinian **veridade** but Spanish **verdad**, Italian **verità**, French **vérité**. Final vowel elision is especially prevalent in France, Catalonia, Switzerland and Romania: Vulgar Latin ***arte** /ˈar.te/ becomes French **art** /aʁ/, Romansh **art** /art/ but Italian **arte** /ˈar.te/, Brazilian Portuguese **arte** /ˈaχ.tʃi/.

In words that have lost their endings, a former penultimate stress now falls on the final syllable: Vulgar Latin ***etate** /eˈtate/ > Spanish **edad** /eˈðað/, Latin **cantāvit** /kanˈtaːwit/ > Romanian **cântă** /kɨnˈtə/. This final stress is the norm in French, which has lost the final syllables of Vulgar Latin: ***prosperu** /ˈprosperu/ *prosperous* >

French **prospère** /pʁɔ'spɛʁ/, ***republica** /re'publika/ *republic* > **république** /ʁepy'blik/.

Languages may also lose unstressed syllables in the middle of a word: Latin **populum** /'populũ/ *people* > ***poplu** > Spanish **pueblo**. Combined with the loss of final syllables, this change pushes Romance towards consistent penultimate or even ultimate stress: Vulgar Latin ***populu** *people* > ***poplu** > French **peuple** /pøpl/, Vulgar Latin ***monumentu** /monu'mentu/ *memorial* > Romanian **mormînt** /mor'mint/ *grave*, Vulgar Latin ***anima** /'anima/ *soul* > ***anma** > Spanish **alma**. Italian, Corsican and Sardinian regularly keep unstressed syllables: Vulgar Latin ***populu** > Italian **popolo** and ***anima** > **anima** but ***domina** /'domina/ *lady* > ***domna** > Italian **donna**.

Quick Tour of Vulgar Latin Grammar

This chapter picks out a few key features of Vulgar Latin grammar. The Vulgar Latin examples are conjectured reconstructions based on common features of the Romance languages, so they represent general historical trends rather than documented speech. This guide simplifies features, explores no feature in depth and provides no comparisons to the modern Romance lanugages. Those details are the subject of the rest of this book.

NOUNS

Every noun in Classical Latin belonged to the masculine, feminine or neuter gender. Vulgar Latin combined the masculine and neuter genders. It distinguished masculine nouns from feminine nouns.

gender	Romance	translation
feminine	*casa	*house*
	*veritate	*truth*
masculine	*pop(u)lu	*people*
	*omine	*man*

Unlike speakers of Classical Latin, Vulgar Latin speakers used definite and indefinite articles with the noun.

Vulgar Latin	*una casa	*a house*
	*illa veritate	*the truth*

Vulgar Latin formed a basic noun from the Classical Latin accusative case.

Latin	veritas	veritatem
Vulgar Latin	*illa veritate	*illa veritate
	the truth (subject)	*the truth* (object)

Vulgar Latin formed <u>plural</u> nouns from the classical accusative plural in the West but the <u>nominative</u> plural in the East.

case	Romance	translation	distribution
nominative plural	*illi populi	*the peoples*	Italy, Romania, Corsica, Dalmatia
accusative plural	*illos populos	*the peoples*	Iberia, France, Switzerland, Sardinia

Speakers employed <u>prepositions</u> where Classical Latin had accusative, dative, genitive and ablative noun <u>cases</u>.

Vulgar Latin	*in illa casa	*in the house*
	*de illa veritate	*of the truth*

The use of cases versus analytic phrases varied between eras, regions, speakers and situations. As a rule of thumb, more popular registers erased the distinction between cases, while more refined registers continued to use noun cases.

Popular Latin	*illa porta de illa casa	*the door of the house*
Late Latin	porta casae	*[the] house's door*

ADJECTIVES

<u>Adjectives</u> normally followed the modified noun.

Vulgar Latin	*illa porta magna	*the big door*

Adjectives matched the gender (masculine or feminine) and number (singular or plural) of the described noun.

Vulgar Latin	*illu omine magnu	*the big man*
	*illos omines magnos	*the big men*
	*illa casa magna	*the big house*
	*illas casas magnas	*the big houses*

Vulgar Latin speakers formed the <u>comparative</u> and <u>superlative</u> with words for *more* instead of the traditional adjective endings.

| Vulgar Latin | ***plus magnu** | *bigger* |
| | ***mais magnu** | *bigger* |

PRONOUNS

Vulgar Latin had nominative (<u>subject</u>), accusative (<u>direct object</u>) and dative (<u>indirect object</u>) forms of six <u>personal pronouns</u>.

Vulgar Latin	***ego**	*I*	(subject)
	*me	*me*	(direct object)
	*mi	*to me*	(indirect object)

Vulgar Latin also had personal <u>possessives</u>, which worked like adjectives or articles.

| Vulgar Latin | ***mea casa** | *my house* |
| | ***meu poplu** | *my people* |

Vulgar Latin employed a variety of <u>interrogative</u>, <u>demonstrative</u> and <u>relative</u> pronouns. Below are some examples.

Vulgar Latin	translation	function
*istu	*this*	demonstrative
*quale	*which*	interrogative
*qui	*who*	interrogative
*illu quale / *illu quid	*that which*	relative
*quod	*that / because*	relative

VERBS

Like the Classical Latin verbs that preceded them, Vulgar Latin <u>verbs</u> had <u>finite</u> forms that took one of six personal endings.

Vulgar Latin	***ego scribo**	*I write*
	*tu scribes	*you write*
	*ille scribet	*he writes*
	*nos scribemus	*we write*

*vos scribetis	*you all write*
*illi scribent	*they write*

The verb endings clearly indicated the <u>subject</u> of the verb. As in Classical Latin, Vulgar Latin normally dropped the subject pronoun.

Vulgar Latin	***scribo**	*I write*
	*scribes	*you write*
	*scribent	*they write*
	*amo	*I love*
	*amas	*you love*
	*amant	*they love*

Verb endings changed between <u>tenses</u>, like present versus past.

Vulgar Latin	***amo**	*I love*
	*amai	*I loved*
	*amas	*you love*
	*amasti	*you loved*

Verb endings changed between <u>moods</u>, such as the indicative (factual) or the subjunctive (contrary to fact).

mood	example	translation
indicative	***dicet quod scribes**	*he says that you are writing*
subjunctive	***dicet quod scribas**	*he says that you should write* (*he tells you to write*)

Vulgar Latin verbs also took <u>non-finite</u> endings that did not inherently refer to a subject.

verb form	example	translation
infinitive	***scribere**	*to write*
past participle	***scriptu**	*written*
gerund	***scribendu**	*writing*

Speakers reduced the four vowel classes of Latin verbs to three or even two <u>thematic vowels</u>.

thematic vowel	example	translation
a	*am-are	*to love*
	*am-as	*you love*
e	*scrib-ere	*to write*
	*scrib-es	*you write*
i	*fin-ire	*to finish*
	*fin-is	*you finish*

Some verbs, including <u>modal</u> verbs, were typically followed by an infinitive.

Vulgar Latin	*potes	*you can*
	*potes scribere	*you can write*

SENTENCES

Vulgar Latin placed <u>subjects</u> before the <u>verb</u> and <u>objects</u> after the verb, but also allowed flexibility in this word order.

Vulgar Latin	*Anna scribet illa littera.	*Anna writes the letter.*
	*Anna abet (una) casa.	*Anna has a house.*
	*Anna casa abet.	*Anna has a house.*
	*casa abet Anna.	*Anna has a house.*

Eventually, Vulgar Latin speakers relied on basic (historically <u>accusative</u>) forms for both subject and object <u>nouns</u>.

Latin	translation	notes
*illu omine dicet illa veritate	*the man tells the truth*	Vulgar: accusative subject, accusative object
*ille omo dicet illa veritate	*the man tells the truth*	Vulgar: nominative subject, accusative object
homo dicit veritatem	*[the] man tells [the] truth*	Classical: nominative subject, accusative object
*hominem dicit veritatem	*[the] man tells [the] truth*	Classical: accusative subject, accusative object (avoided)

When object <u>pronouns</u> were used, the pronouns preceded the main verb.

Vulgar Latin	*tu amas Anna	*you love Anna*
	*Anna amat Paulu	*Anna loves Paul*
	*Anna te amat	*Anna loves you*

Speakers initially distinguished <u>indirect object</u> (dative case) pronouns from <u>direct object</u> (accusative case) pronouns.

| Vulgar Latin | *mi dices illa veritate | *you tell the truth to me* |
| | *me vides | *you see me* |

Vulgar Latin <u>passivized</u> verbs with a reflexive pronoun or with *essere *be*. These constructions allowed speakers to avoid the passive endings of Classical Latin.

construction	example	translation	literally
reflexive	*se scribet illa littera		*the letter writes itself*
*essere	*illa littera est scripta	*the letter is written*	*the letter is written*
classical ending	*littera scrib-itur		*[the] letter write-PASSIVE*

Vulgar Latin inherited a straightforward framework for <u>negative</u> and <u>interrogative</u> sentences.

Vulgar Latin	*Illu amas?	*Do you love him?*
	*Illa casa est magna?	*Is the house big?*
	*Non illu amas.	*You do not love him.*
	*Illa casa non est magna.	*The house is not big.*

Speakers could combine multiple verbs with <u>conjunctions</u> and <u>relatives</u> to form longer sentences.

| Vulgar Latin | *Scribet et cantat. | *She writes and she sings.* |
| | *Scio quod scribes illa littera. | *I know that you're writing the letter.* |

Language Names, Groups & Maps

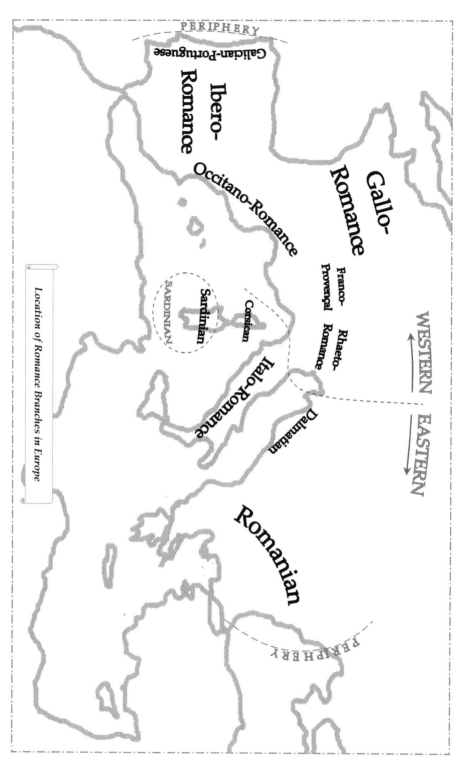

Location of Romance Branches in Europe

PERIPHERY

Galician-Portuguese

Ibero-Romance

Gallo-Romance

Occitano-Romance

Franco-Provençal

Rhaeto-Romance

SARDINIAN

Sardinian

Corsican

Italo-Romance

Dalmatian

WESTERN

EASTERN

Romanian

PERIPHERY

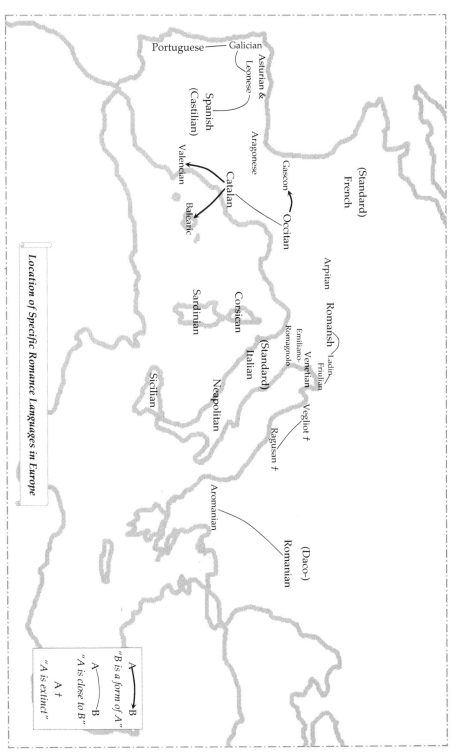

Location of Specific Romance Languages in Europe

Portuguese — Galician
Asturian & Leonese
Spanish (Castilian)
Aragonese
Gascon
Occitan
Catalan
Valencian
Balearic
(Standard) French
Arpitan
Romansh — Ladin
Emiliano-Romagnolo
Venetian
Friulian
Vegliot †
Ragusan †
Sardinian
Corsican
(Standard) Italian
Neapolitan
Sicilian
Aromanian
(Daco-) Romanian

A ——→ B   "B is a form of A"
A ←— B   "A is close to B"
A †   "A is extinct"

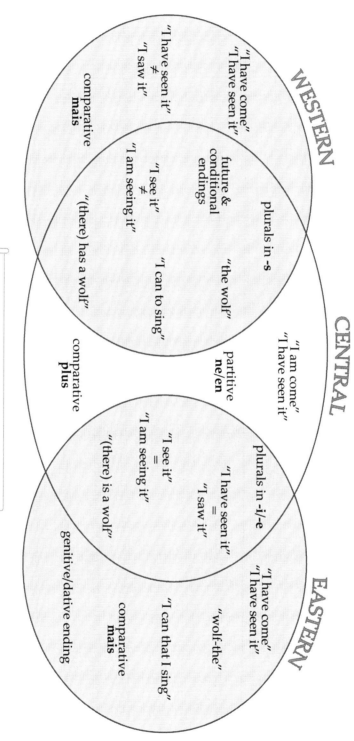

Romance Languages across Grammatical Space

GLOSSARY OF LANGUAGE NAMES

Aragonese: a distinct language spoken in Northern Spain.

Asturian and Leonese, Astur-Leonese: a continuum of closely related dialects spoken in Northern Spain.

Catalan and Occitan, Occitano-Romance: related Romance languages spoken in Southern France and Eastern Spain.

Catalan and Valencian: a dialect continuum in Eastern Spain with close affinities to Occitan and more distant relations to French and Spanish.

Central Romance: the Romance languages spoken in and near Italy, especially where their features differ from Western Romance and Eastern Romance.

conversational: words or structures found in everyday speech but perhaps not in writing.

Corsican: the language native to the northernmost of the two major Tyrrhenian islands, spoken to the north of Sardinian.

Dalmatian: an extinct Romance language once spoken along the eastern coast of the Adriatic.

Eastern Romance: the Romance languages east of Southern Italy.

Emiliano-Romagnolo: a group of closely related languages and dialects spoken in Northern Italy.

Extremaduran: regional language of southwestern Spain with close affinities to Asturian and Leonese.

Franco-Provençal, Arpitan: dialects native to southeastern France, which differ from the langues d'oc and langues d'oïl.

French languages, Gallo-Romance: the Romance languages of France.

Friulian: a Rhaeto-Romance language spoken in Northern Italy that shares many features with Ladin.

Galician and Portuguese, Galician-Portuguese: a subfamily of closely related languages in Western Iberia.

Iberian languages, Ibero-Romance: the Romance languages of Spain and Portugal.

Italo-Romance: the Romance languages of Italy.

Ladin: a distinct Rhaeto-Romance language spoken in Northern Italy.

Langues d'oc: a dialect continuum in Southern France, here grouped together as dialects of Occitan.

Langues d'oïl: historical Romance dialect continuum in Northern France, now mainly represented by French.

Late Latin: the continued use of formal and written Latin from Late Antiquity to the Middle Ages.

literary: words limited to written works and typically associated with prestigious or educated registers.

Neapolitan: narrowly, the local language of Naples, but broadly including the variants of Neapolitan and Calabrian in Southern Italy.

Northern Italian: languages of Northern Italy, which broadly share much in common with Western Romance.

Occitan: the langues d'oc of Southern France.

Old X (Old French, Old Spanish, etc.): medieval or premodern forms of a specific language.

periphery, Romance periphery, languages along the periphery: the Romance languages most distant from Rome, especially Iberian (such as Portuguese) and Romanian (such as Standard Romanian).

Rhaeto-Romance, Rhaetian: a diverse collection of languages and dialects native to Switzerland and surrounding areas.

Romance languages, Romance, pan-Romance, all languages: used interchangeably to refer to features found in every (or almost every) Romance language.

Romanian languages: a number of closely related Romance languages and dialects spoken in Eastern Europe, including Daco-Romanian, Aromanian and Istro-Romanian.

Romansh: a collection of closely related Rhaeto-Romance dialects spoken in Switzerland.

Sardinian: a collection of dialects native to Sardinia, which represent a completely separate branch of Romance.

Sicilian: the regional language of Sicily in Southern Italy.

Southern Italian: languages of Southern Italy, which broadly differ from the languages of Northern Italy, France, Switzerland and Spain but share common features with Eastern Romance.

Swiss Romance, Swiss languages: synonymous here with Rhaeto-Romance.

Venetian: a distinct language native to Northern Italy.

Vulgar Latin: the popular forms of Latin, including but not limited to the common parent varieties of the modern Romance languages.

Western Romance: the Romance languages west of Northern Italy.

Western versus Eastern Romance: a way of grouping and contrasting languages based on broad regional commonalities. For instance, the Romance languages of Switzerland, France, Spain and Portugal form plural nouns with **-s**, but Italian, Dalmatian and Romanian have plural nouns that end in a vowel.

Suggested Resources

GENERAL

- Wikipedia has many healthy articles on the grammar and phonology of specific Romance languages. You'll also find wikis in Latin and quite a few of the lesser-known languages: http://www.wikipedia.org.

- The Wiktionary community focuses on vocabulary items and grammar tables: www.wiktionary.org, fr.wiktionary.org (French), an.wiktionary.org (Aragonese), scn.wiktionary.org (Sicilian), roa-rup.wiktionary.org (Aromanian), it.wiktionary.org (Italian), etc.

- Regularly updated multilingual dictionaries with examples and discussion boards for a number of Romance languages: http://www.wordreference.com.

- Dictionaries for many languages: http://www.lexilogos.com.

- Verbs conjugated in many languages: http://www.verbix.com.

- This book's home site offers an online version of this Romance grammar, along with lessons on linguistics for language learners: nativlang.com/linguistics/, nativlang.com/romance-languages/.

VULGAR LATIN & COMMON ROMANCE

- Allen, W. Sydney. *Vox Latina*. Cambridge: Cambridge University Press, 1978.

- Boyd-Bowman, Peter. *From Latin to Romance in Sound Charts*. Georgetown: Georgetown University Press, 1980.

- Buchi, Éva and Wolfgang Schweickard (dir.). *Dictionnaire Étymologique Roman (DÉRom)*. Nancy: ATILF, 2008. http://www.atilf.fr/DERom.

- Harris, Martin and Nigel Vincent. *The Romance Languages*. New York: Oxford University Press, 1988.

- Herman, Jószef. *Vulgar Latin*. University Park, PA: Pennsylvania State University Press, 2000.

- Solodow, Joseph B. *Latin Alive*. New York: Cambridge University Press, 2010.

SPECIFIC LANGUAGES

You can choose from among a mountain of materials to study the more popular languages (Spanish, French, Portuguese, Italian and Classical Latin). Below I list helpful resources for some of the less-studied Romance languages.

It's also worth checking out the general resources above, since they share information about these languages. What's more, if you don't require much handholding, you can also start mining the internet for examples. Webpages exist in many of the "smaller" Romance languages.

Galician
- Seminario de Lingüística Informática. *Diccionario CLUVI Inglés-Galego*. Last modified in 2012. http://sli.uvigo.es/CLIG/.

Asturian
- Academia de la Llingua Asturiana. *Gramática de la Llingua Asturiana*. Oviedo: Academia de la Llingua Asturiana, 2001.

- García Arias, Xosé Lluis. *Diccionario general de la lengua asturiana*. Accessed March 27, 2012. http://mas.lne.es/diccionario/.

Aragonese
- Segura Malagón, Juan José. "Descripción gramatical sincrónica." Last modified in 2010. http://www.charrando.com/info.php.

- Gil, Antón-Chusé. "Notes for a Grammar of Aragonese." Last modified in 1997. http://sapiens.ya.com/qkrachas/gramarang/gramatica.html.

Catalan

- *Catalan Dictionary*. New York: Routledge, 2000.

- Institut d'Estudis Catalans. *Gramàtica de la llengua catalana*. Accessed March 27, 2012. http://www2.iec.cat/institucio/seccions/Filologica/gramatica/.

- Wheeler et al. *Catalan: A Comprehensive Grammar*. London: Routledge, 1999.

Occitan

- PanOccitan. *Le dictionnaire Occitan-Français*. Accessed March 27, 2012. http://www.panoccitan.org/diccionari.aspx.

Old French

- Études Littéraires. "Ancien français." Last modified January 2012. http://www.etudes-litteraires.com/ancien-francais.php.

- Linguistics Research Center. "Old French Online: Series Introduction." Last modified August 11, 2011. http://www.utexas.edu/cola/centers/lrc/eieol/ofrol-0-X.html.

Arpitan

- Freelang.com. "Dictionnaire en ligne Arpitan savoyard." Last modified September 18, 2011. http://www.freelang.com/dictionnaire/arpitan_savoyard.php.

- Région Autonome Vallée d'Aoste: Assessorat de l'Éducation et de la Culture. "Apprendre le francoprovençal." Accessed March 27, 2012. http://www.patoisvda.org/gna/index.cfm/francoprovencal-apprendre-patois.html.

Romagnolo

- Maioli, Marcello. *Corso multimediale di dialetto romagnolo.* Accessed March 27, 2012. http://marcelpachiot.altervista.org.

Romansh

- Caduff et al. *Grammatica per l'instrucziun dal rumantsch grischun.* Freiburg University, 2009.

- Lia Rumantscha. *Pledari Grond.* Last modified January 27, 2012. http://www.pledarigrond.ch.

- myPledari Project. *myPledari.* Accessed March 27, 2012. http://www.pledari.ch.

Ladin

- Soravia, Giancarlo. *Ladino Cadorino di Venas.* Last modified September 11, 2007. http://ladin-cadorin.blogspot.com.

Venetian

- Brunelli, Michelle. *Dizsionario Generałe de ła Łéngua Vèneta e łe só varianti.* Last modified December 8, 2006. http://www.dizsionario.org.

Corsican

- *A lingua corsa.* Last modified April 26, 2009. http://gbatti-alinguacorsa.pagesperso-orange.fr.

Sardinian

- Lepori, Antonio. *Compendio di grammatica campidanese per italofoni.* Quartu Sant'Elena, Sardinia: Edizioni C.R., 2001.

- Puddu, Mario. *Ditzionàriu Online.* Accessed March 27, 2012. http://www.ditzionariu.org.

Neapolitan

- Argenziano, Salvatore. *La Grammatica di Torrese*. Last modified in 2002. http://www.torreomnia.com/Testi/argenziano/dizionario/grammatica1.htm.

- Wikibooks. *The Neapolitan Wikiprimer*. Last modified January 6, 2012. http://en.wikibooks.org/wiki/Neapolitan.

Sicilian

- Lingua Siciliana. "Sicilian Grammar in English." Last modified February 17, 2008. http://www.linguasiciliana.org/category/cursu-sicilianu/sicilian-grammar-in-english-inglisi/.

Dalmatian

- *Dalmatian Language*. Accessed March 27, 2012. http://dalmatianlanguage.yolasite.com.

Aromanian or "Vlach"

- Cunia, Tiberius. *Dictsiunar a Limbãljei Armãneascã*. Editura Cartea Aromãnã, 2010.

Romanian

- Gönczöl, Ramona. *Romanian: An Essential Grammar*. London: Routledge, 2008.

- Cojocaru, Dana. *Romanian Grammar*. Accessed March 27, 2012. http://www.seelrc.org:8080/grammar/mainframe.jsp?nLanguageID=5.

Index

be. *See* essere
betg (Romansh), 110, 208
bosté (Sardinian). *See* politeness
ça (French). *See* neuter pronouns
că (Romanian). *See* quod
case, 19, 120
    accusative nouns, 19
    accusative pronouns, 78
    dative pronouns, 79
    genitive & dative nouns, 23
    nominative nouns, 20
    nominative pronouns, 73
    vocative nouns, 23
cel (Romanian), 94
che (Italian). *See* quod
clauses. *See* main clauses,
    dependent clauses
clitics
    locative, 107, 220
    object pronouns, 78–79, 106,
        133, 134, 219
    partitive, 107, 220
    prepositions, 97
    subject pronouns, 76, 104
cognates, 14, 22
collective neuter, 13, 18, 122
comin(i)tiare ad, 69
commands (with verb), 49
comparative adjectives, 93, 206
complex sentences, 113
compound sentences, 113
conditional mood, 50, 115, 191–98
configurations. *See* word orders
conjugations, 38
conjunctions, 98
conmigo (Iberian), 132
consecutio temporum, 114

consonant clusters, 226
consonants, 226
    lenition of, 228
    palatalization of, 227
copula, 54
cun megus (Sardinian), 132
dative case
    nouns in the, 23
    pronouns in the, 79
de, 28
    comparative, 93, 206
    partitive, 29
    possessive, 23, 103
debere, 59, 192
decât (Romanian), 93
default gender, 75, 77, 92, 95
default word order. *See* word
    orders
definite articles, 24, 125, 127, 129
deixis. *See* distance
deletion, 230
demonstratives
    adjectives, 85, 102
    pronouns, 85
    syntax, 101
dependent clauses, 114, 213
derivation, 14, 39
determiners
    articles, 24
    demonstratives, 101
    indefinites, 87
    interrogatives, 102
    possessives, 83, 102
diminutives, 15
diphthongs, 225
direct object. *See* objects
distance

specifiers. *See* determiners,
    auxiliaries, etc.
stare, 54
    progressive aspect with, 63
stem
    of adjectives, 90
    of nouns, 8, 10
    of verbs, 37
stem-changing verbs, 40
stress accent, 229
strong object pronouns, 82, 132
subjects
    passive, 116, 221
    pronominal, 72, 104, 130
    verbal, 104
subjunctive mood, 47, 167–74
    instead of imperative, 48
    versus indicative, 47
subordinate clauses, 114, 213, *See*
    dependent clauses
superlative adjectives, 93
syllables, 229
syntax
    adjectives, 100, 203–4
    adverbs, 94
    affirmative sentences, 109, 207
    commands, 113, 216
    comparatives & superlatives,
        93, 206
    compound sentences, 113
    conjunctions, 98
    de+noun, 103
    hypotheticals, 115
    infinitives after finites, 115, 215
    negation, 110, 208
    noun phrases, 100, 203–5, 205

object pronouns, 106, 107, 134,
    219
particles, 97
passives, 116, 221
possessives, 23, 103, 205
prepositional phrases, 97
pro-drop, 33, 35, 104
sequence of tenses & moods,
    114
subject pronouns, 104
subjunctive after quod, 114,
    214
thematic roles, 108
transitivity, 105, 134
verb phrases, 104, 107, 134
wh-questions, 112, 211
yes-no questions, 111, 212
tenere, 52
    idiomatic expressions with, 61
tense & aspect, 37, 42
tenses, 37
    future, 43, 159–66
    imperfect, 42, 151–58
    near future, 66
    past (preterit), 40, 143–50
    perfect, 56
    pluperfect, 59
    present, 39, 135–42
    simple/historic past. *See* past
        (preterit)
thematic roles, 108
thematic vowels, 38
third conjugation. *See*
    conjugations
third person. *See* person
transitive verbs, 105
tu. *See* subject pronouns

65674889R00147

Made in the USA
Charleston, SC
28 December 2016